1981

Selected Poems of
ANTONIO MACHADO

Selected Poems of

ANTONIO MACHADO

Translated and with an Introduction by
BETTY JEAN CRAIGE

LOUISIANA STATE UNIVERSITY PRESS
Baton Rouge & London

Design: Dwight Agner
Typeface: VIP Aster
Composition: Graphic Composition, Inc.
Printing: Thomson-Shore, Inc.
Binding: John H. Dekker & Sons, Inc.

LIBRARY OF CONGRESS CATALOGING IN PUBLICATION DATA

Machado y Ruiz, Antonio, 1875–1939.
    Selected poems of Antonio Machado.

    I. Craige, Betty Jean. II. Title.
PQ6623.A3A245   1978   861'.6'2   78–57504
ISBN 0–8071–0456–6

For Craige, Branch, and Wren—
and their parents

INDICE

CONTENTS

ACKNOWLEDGMENTS

I WOULD like to thank Carlos Kussrow-Corma for his kind help in the interpretation of a few of Machado's most difficult poems, Wilder P. Scott and James B. Colvert for their intelligent assistance in proofreading, and Calvin Brown, Steven Hale, Sheila Bailey, Carolyn Clutter, and Ginny Munnell for their help in the preparation of the final manuscript. I also wish to express my appreciation to don José Rollán Riesco for his authorization as representative of the heirs of Antonio Machado to reprint the Spanish poems. And finally I thank my editor, Marie Jones, for putting up with my last-minute changes on some of the translations, changes I wanted to make every time I looked at the poetry.

INTRODUCTION

Antonio Machado

I was born in Seville one night in July of 1875, in the famous palace of the Dueñas, situated on the street of the same name.

My memories of my birthplace are all from childhood, for at the age of eight I went to Madrid, where my parents moved, and I was educated at the Institución Libre de Enseñanza. I still have a lively affection and deep gratitude for its teachers. My adolescence and my youth were spent in Madrid. I have traveled some through France and Spain. In 1907 I obtained a professorship of French, which I held for five years in Soria. There I married; there died my wife, whose memory accompanies me always. I moved to Baeza, where I live today. My hobbies are taking walks and reading.

1917

From Madrid to Paris at the age of twenty-four (1899). Paris was still the city of the "Dreyfus affair" in politics, of symbolism in poetry, of impressionism in painting, of elegant skepticism in criticism. I knew Oscar Wilde and Jean Moréas personally. The great sacred literary figure was Anatole France.

From Madrid to Paris (1902). During this year in Paris I met Rubén Darío.

From 1903 to 1910, various trips through Spain: Granada, Córdoba, the land of Soria, the source of the Duero, the cities of Castile, Valencia, Aragón.

From Soria to Paris (1910). I attended a course of Henri Bergson at the College of France.

From 1912 to 1919, from Baeza to the source of the Guadalquivir and to almost all the cities of Andalucía.

Since 1919 I spend approximately half of my time in Segovia and the other half in Madrid. My latest trips have been to Avila, León, Palencia, and Barcelona (1928).

1931

Modern Spanish literature came to birth with the "Generation of 1898," which rose out of Spain's defeat in the Spanish-American War. In the sudden recognition which followed failure Unamuno called for a new subjectivism for Spanish intellectuals in his essay "¡Adentro!", to which the other young writers of the decade—Azorín, Pio Baroja, Juan Ramón Jiménez, Ramón del Valle Inclán, Manuel and Antonio Machado—responded. Their eyes turned inward, to Spain, its history and its destiny; to the character of the Spaniard and his God; to the timeless Spanish question of dream and reality; to themselves. Their literature became subjective, lyrical, philosophical.

Of these early twentieth-century literary figures, Unamuno is perhaps the giant, the philosopher-poet-novelist best known outside his own country; but after Unamuno, Machado has come to be respected as one of Spain's great poets, an influence on those to follow. For Machado began as an intensely lyrical poet in the tradition of the French symbolists, then turned outward to look at his own land and people, and finally arrived at a position which may be called existentialist, because of his view of man as a being in time, his agnosticism, and his dread of nothingness.

Antonio Machado was a pensive, solitary man who preferred the peace of the ancient towns of the provinces to the excitement of the literary circles of Madrid. Having passed his adolescence in Spain's capital, Machado moved to Soria at the age of thirty-two, to spend five years in that "land of Castile" teaching French in a secondary school. As he says in his brief autobiographical note, there he married (a sixteen-year-old girl named Leonor), and there he lost his young bride, who died two years later of tuberculosis.

Machado's love for Leonor and her death was the great tragedy of his life from which he felt he would not recover. After this experience he turned to philosophy (while continuing to teach French and Spanish literature in the cities of Baeza and Segovia), and with philosophy to prose, as an appropriate form for the expression of his thought. In the late 1920s he began participating in the literary life of Madrid by collaborating with his brother Manuel in the production of many Spanish Golden Age plays and a few plays of their own. It was during this period that Machado met and fell in love with a mysterious woman who appears in his late poetry as "Guiomar."

In the years between 1927, when he was elected to the Spanish Academy, and the outbreak of the Spanish Civil War, Machado involved himself in writing articles in support of the Republicans; and when the Rightist forces under Franco defeated the Republicans in 1939, the poet fled to Collioure, France, where he died in February. There Antonio Machado is buried.

His Poetry

We are victims—I thought—of a double illusion. If we look outside and endeavor to penetrate things, our external world loses its solidity, and ends up dissolving in front of us when we arrive at the belief that it does not exist in itself, but only through us. But if, convinced of the intimate reality, we look inside, then everything appears to us to come from outside, and it is our internal world, ourselves, which disintegrates. What is there to do then? To weave the thread that we are given, to dream our dream, to live; only in this way shall we be able to work the miracle of the generation. A man attentive to himself and attempting to listen to himself drowns the only voice that he would be able to hear: his own; but foreign noises bewilder him. Then will we be mere spectators of the world? But our eyes are laden with reason, and reason analyzes and dissolves. Soon we shall see the theater in ruins, and, finally, our solitary shadow projected on the scene.

from Prologue to *Land of Castile*, 1917

The dilemma of "subjectivism" or "objectivism" with which Machado wrestled throughout his life is central to the form his writing takes in the course of its evolution. There is a movement from a solipsistic expression of the "I" in *Solitudes* through a recovery of external reality in *Land of Castile*, in which the poet turns away from his inner world and begins to look outside himself, to the disappearance of the "I" in the ironic prose of *Juan de Mairena* and *Abel Martín*, where Machado speaks through the mouths of "apocryphal" philosophers. Thus dramatic dialogue, in which Machado as poet is absent, gradually takes the place of lyricism, as irony comes to dominate the poet's attitude toward life. Increasing skepticism and the existential awareness of the *nada* eventually permit neither faith in his own subjective reality nor faith in any objective reality; and finally Machado can express his own ideas only in the form of questions, or through ironic humor, or by way of poetry written by a character he invents.

Machado published in 1903 a little volume of poems entitled *Solitudes*, which four years later he expanded and reissued under the name of *Solitudes, Galleries, and Other Poems*. During this period, as he says in its Prologue, Machado conceived of poetry as "a deep palpitation of the spirit," what the soul says "with its own voice, in animated response to the contact with the world." The poetry is indeed lyrical—lyricism being the voice of the subjectivity—and is an expression of the poet's journey into himself, in his "solitude," into his memory, through "dreaming."

The world of *Solitudes* is a world of white courtyards, bubbling fountains, the scent of lemon and orange trees, and the warm haze of late afternoon that moves the poet to dreams. For Machado, dreaming is an active state of reverie in which he evokes and elaborates the past or transforms the present into the truth of his inner reality. The water flowing from the fountain is heard in the rhythm of the poetry which expresses the poet's inner consciousness of the rhythm of human existence; the fountain spills forth its water as the poet dreams, as time flows. The setting sun is an emblem of death, and its warm rays color the landscape as the poet's nostalgia floods the poems. There is a hush in the air, even when children's voices rise from the plaza where they are playing. And the poet is alone, hearing the sounds of his childhood, the ancient, unchanging rhythms of life.

As Machado states in the Prologue to *Land of Castile*, this volume represents his rejection of subjectivism and his new acceptance of objective reality. His concerns shift from the galleries of his dreams and their fleeting figures to the banks of the Duero and the Spanish peasant, from the search for his personal lost past to a preoccupation with the future of Spain. Machado defined poetry as "dialogue of man with time" and "the essential word in time"; and the radical reorientation evident in *Land of Castile* reveals that the "time" with which he now maintains his dialogue is no longer the Bergsonian subjective time of his private inner reality, but rather the historical time of his present existence in a particular place, at a particular moment.

The implications of Machado's turning outward are felt in the rhythm, themes, and structure of the poetry of *Land of Castile*. Because the poet is looking to the world outside himself for the essential rhythms of human existence, the incantatory rhythm of many of the earlier poems, in which the poet's inner life merges with the monotonous rhythm of the eternally flowing fountain, disappears. Discarding the private lyricism of *Solitudes*, Machado now employs many of the traditional, anonymous verse forms of popular Spanish poetry, including the octosyllabic "romance" form, in which he writes *The Land of Alvargonzález*. This "new romance," he says, "does not emanate from the narratives of heroic deeds, but of the land where they were sung," and its "heroes" are peasants reenacting the archetypal myth of Cain and Abel.

The general change in form from lyrical to more narrative poetry, expressive of Machado's new attitude towards the world, reflects a social awakening in the poet. As Machado says much later (in the character of Jorge Meneses in *Juan de Mairena*), "Modern lyricism, from the decline of Romanticism to our time (that of symbolism), is perhaps a luxury, somewhat abusive, of the Manchesterian man, of bourgeois individualism, based on private property. The poet exhibits his heart with the boasting of the rich bourgeois who shows off his palaces, his coaches, his horses, and his mistresses. The heart of the poet, so rich in sonorities, is almost an insult to the hearty toneless voice of the masses, enslaved by mechanical labor." The private symbolism of fountains and galleries born of the poet's early extreme isolation yields to more "public" symbolism, references to history and myth, references to what is peculiar to Spain, references intelligible to the whole Spanish community on a conscious level. Machado now recognizes man's natural ties with the earth, and he sees the various types that constitute the community of mankind—the madman, the criminal, the peasant. He looks into the austere face of the rugged Castilian for the secret of the Spanish God; he looks across the rugged face of the land for the secret of Spain's destiny.

It is this Machado, the Machado whose sympathies lie with the peasants tilling the soil and later with the Republican forces seeking reform of the unjust social system of Spain, whom José María Castellet hails as the forerunner of the new (post-Civil War) Spanish poetry. For Machado has converted from the tradition of symbolism, in which he is the solitary poet isolated from the rest of mankind hearkening to the rhythms of his own private soul, to what perhaps could be called the tradition of historical realism (in some of the poetry of *Land of Castile*), in which the poet is the voice of the people and speaks to a particular historical situation. The history of Spanish poetry in the twentieth century is an account of a general reorientation of this nature occurring in the 1930s as a result, in part, of the worldwide depression and the Spanish Civil War. Machado was twenty years ahead of his time.[1]

Machado's spiritual evolution[2] from solipsism to a recognition of the world outside his consciousness can be traced through the changing dialogue form, which he employs throughout his poetry. In *Solitudes*, his most lyrical work, Machado engages in dialogue (in the familiar *tú*) with the fountain, the mysterious figures of his "soul," the afternoon or evening, the morning, the night; since nature mirrors his subjective state in this book, Machado is speaking to various aspects of his self, his "soul." In *Land of Castile*, however, when he moves to Soria and marries, the *tú* is the arid land, Spain, the oak, the Guadarrama, Soria, and his lost bride (who died in 1912); so here he is addressing the world outside himself. Later Machado turns to witty aphorisms for the expression of his ideas and finally to philosophical prose in which he himself is absent. In *Abel Martín* and *Juan de Mairena* the dialogue is between "apocryphal" professors and students, and the poetry interspersed in the dialogue is by "apocryphal" poets.

The irony in the structure of this late writing, as well as in its actual content, implies doubt: doubt of self, doubt of the meaningfulness of existence, doubt of God. When the poet is besieged by doubt, such that his self is divided—the conceptual, critical self seeing the intuitive, lyrical self at a distance—then lyricism, which implies *one* voice, is no longer adequate. The self-mockery demands another form: the fragments of prose dialogue through which Machado may put forth his ideas tentatively and with humor, ideas for which he may disclaim responsibility, since they belong to the characters he has created. The beautiful lyrics to Guiomar are found in Abel Martín's "Apocryphal Songbook." It is to this ironic distance of poet from poem that Machado's journey away from subjectivism has taken him.

The late poems, many of them composed, says Machado, by

1. See José María Castellet, *Un Cuarto de siglo de poesía española (1939–1964)* (Barcelona: Editorial Seix Barral, S.A., 1966), 35–66.

2. See José María Valverde's excellent article, "Evolución del sentido espiritual de la obra de Antonio Machado," (*Cuadernos Hispanoamericanos* (Madrid), 1949, nos. 11–12, pp 399–414).

Abel Martín, reflect a profound existential pessimism, the essence of which is expressed in the sonnet "To the Great Zero."

> When the *Being Who Is* made nothingness,
> and rested, for so he deserved,
> then the day had night and darkness,
> and man company in the absence of his love.

> *Fiat umbra!* Human consciousness was born.
> And the universal egg rose, and was known to man,
> who held it, empty, cold, forlorn,
> full of weightless mist, in his hand.

> Take the integral zero, the hollow sphere,
> and face it, standing tall, that it be in your vision.
> Because the wild beast's back has become your shoulder,

> and because it is the miracle of being without completion,
> offer up today, poet, a song from the frontier
> to death, to silence, and to oblivion.

"Let there be darkness!" says the "Being Who Is," and human consciousness is born—the awareness of absence, of emptiness, of incompletion. This is what it is to be man: to stand tall, in the face of nothingness, and drink a toast to death, silence, and oblivion.

The Translation

The poetry of Antonio Machado is a quiet poetry, reflecting the man behind it whose favorite hour was the late afternoon and whose favorite pastime was walking through ancient streets into the peaceful countryside. The language is rhythmical and simple, the vocabulary that of a man who loved nature. Machado's touch is light—visually and aurally—from his early *Solitudes* echoing Verlaine's "de la musique avant toute chose" to his late sonnets in *From an Apocryphal Songbook* full of existential despair. Machado suggests; the reader understands the rest. In this translation I have endeavored above all to communicate the feeling of Machado's poetry—its rhythm, its tone, its understatement.

For Machado, poetry is "the word in time"; and, as Juan de Mairena says, an excellent device for putting the word into time is rhyme, "the encounter of one sound with the memory of another." Rhyme and rhythm are essential to Machado's poetry, which aspires (again in the words of Mairena) to "eternalize time." However, what is important is not the rhyme in itself, but rather the relation of that rhyme to the language in which the poem is written; and it is this relationship which the translator must consider in bringing poetry from one language into another.

The Spanish language rhymes easily, naturally, in such a way that Machado's use of assonance in every other line of an eighteen-line poem, for example, does not leap out at us as the most obvious achievement of the poem. English, on the other hand, does not rhyme easily, and a reproduction of Machado's rhyme scheme in an English translation of that eighteen-line poem could turn the poem into highly contrived eighteenth-century verse. The effect would be entirely different. Therefore, I have attempted everywhere to reproduce the *effect* of the original Spanish poem upon the reader. Where rhyme and rhythm are prominent in the Spanish poem, I have generally employed rhyme and similar rhythm in the English version; but in order to preserve the semblance of natural speech that is characteristic of Machado's verse I have frequently sought off-rhyme and a rhythm perhaps not quite as regular as in the Spanish. The sonnets, since the poet elected to follow that demanding form, I have translated as sonnets.

Certain problems inherent in the language difference cannot ever be solved, and for this reason any translation is a poor imitation of the original poetry. For instance, one vocabulary difficulty encountered here was the translation of the word *tarde*, which for Machado means late afternoon when the sun is close to the horizon or soon after it has set, the hour when he takes his walk. Another word important to Machado and impossible to translate is *caminante*, which has usually been rendered as *wanderer*, although the English word does not embrace *road* (*camino*) or *walking* (*caminar*), as does the Spanish.

Translation of poetry is, finally, an impossibility. The poem has its source not in the intellect but in the dark recesses of man's mind, and that burning intuition, that "deep palpitation of the spirit," rises to the light of the poet's consciousness already clothed in particular images and particular words. To paraphrase Croce, the expression of the vision is the vision; thus a translation of the expression is not, and cannot be, a reproduction of the original vision.

Yet knowledge through "translation" of a thinker who thought in a tongue other than our own is infinitely better than ignorance. The purpose of this book is to introduce to the English-speaking world a poet of the Spanish language whose concerns ranged far beyond the frontiers of his homeland. Machado's journey from symbolism to existentialism (before the philosophy was given its name) takes him to the heart of the modern period, where he speaks for many, standing on the edge of oblivion and facing the darkness:

> With the goblet filled to the brim with shadow,
> with this never full heart,
> let us honor the Lord who made Nothingness
> and in our faith our reason carved.

SOLEDADES
SOLITUDES

I *El viajero*

Está en la sala familiar, sombría,
y entre nosotros, el querido hermano
que en el sueño infantil de un claro día
vimos partir hacia un país lejano.

Hoy tiene ya las sienes plateadas,
un gris mechón sobre la angosta frente;
y la fría inquietud de sus miradas
revela un alma casi toda ausente.

Deshójanse las copas otoñales
del parque mustio y viejo.
La tarde, tras los húmedos cristales,
se pinta, y en el fondo del espejo.

El rostro del hermano se ilumina
suavemente. ¿Floridos desengaños
dorados por la tarde que declina?
¿Ansias de vida nueva en nuevos años?

¿Lamentará la juventud perdida?
Lejos quedó—la pobre loba—muerta.
¿La blanca juventud nunca vivida
teme que ha de cantar ante su puerta?

¿Sonríe al sol de oro
de la tierra de un sueño no encontrada;
y ve su nave hender el mar sonoro,
de viento y luz la blanca vela hinchada?

El ha visto las hojas otoñales,
amarillas, rodar, las olorosas
ramas del eucalipto, los rosales
que enseñan otra vez sus blancas rosas. . .

Y este dolor que añora o desconfía
el temblor de una lágrima reprime,
y un resto de viril hipocresía
en el semblante pálido se imprime.

I *The Traveler*

In the deepening shadows of the den
we are with the brother we loved
who in a child's dream of a clear day
we saw depart for a distant land.

Across his forehead is a lock of gray,
the hair of his temples white;
an almost empty soul shows
in the cold unrest of his eyes.

The leaves drop from withered limbs
of ancient trees in the park.
And on the mirror and misty panes
is painted the dark of fall.

The face of the brother is bright.
Flowered disillusionments of old
colored gold by waning light?
Longings for new life in years to come?

Is he lamenting his lost youth?
That poor wolf—youth—died far away.
Those years of boyhood never lived—
does he fear their howl at his gate?

Is he smiling at the golden sun
of the land of a dream he did not find?
Is he seeing his ship plow the roaring seas,
its white sail filled with light and wind?

He has seen the blowing yellow leaves,
the sweet limbs of the eucalyptus tree
in autumn; he has seen the bush
on which white roses again appear.

And the pain of memory and loss of faith
holds back a solitary tear;
a vestige of virile hypocrisy
marks the pallid face.

Serio retrato en la pared clarea
todavía. Nosotros divagamos.
En la tristeza del hogar golpea
el tictac del reloj. Todos callamos.

III

La plaza y los naranjos encendidos
con sus frutas redondas y risueñas.

Tumulto de pequeños colegiales
que, al salir en desorden de la escuela,
llenan el aire de la plaza en sombra
con la algazara de sus voces nuevas.

¡Alegría infantil en los rincones
de las ciudades muertas! . . .
¡Y algo nuestro de ayer, que todavía
vemos vagar por estas calles viejas!

V *Recuerdo infantil*

Una tarde parda y fría
de invierno. Los colegiales
estudian. Monotonía
de lluvia tras los cristales.

Es la clase. En un cartel
se representa a Caín
fugitivo, y muerto Abel
junto a una mancha carmín.

Con timbre sonoro y hueco
truena el maestro, un anciano
mal vestido, enjuto y seco,
que lleva un libro en la mano.

Y todo un coro infantil
va cantando la lección:
"mil veces ciento, cien mil;
mil veces mil, un millón."

The serious portrait on the wall
grows bright. And we digress.
In the gloom there by the hearth
the clock ticks. All hush.

III

The plaza and the burning orange trees
with their round and smiling fruit.

The tumult of the children
who, tumbling out of school,
fill the air of the shady plaza
with voices noisy, new.

The child's joy in the corners
of the dead cities! . . .
And something of ours from yesterday
we see roaming these ancient streets.

V *Childhood Memory*

A cold afternoon of winter,
gloomy. School children
study. Monotony
of rain on windows.

Class time. On a sign
are pictured fugitive Cain
and Abel dead
beside a crimson stain.

With a loud ringing bell
the teacher calls, an old man
poorly dressed, shriveled, thin,
holding a book in his hand.

And a chorus of children's voices
continues singing the lesson:
"a thousand times a hundred, a hundred thousand;
a thousand times a thousand, one million."

Una tarde parda y fría
de invierno. Los colegiales
estudian. Monotonía
de la lluvia en los cristales.

VI

Fue una clara tarde, triste y soñolienta
tarde de verano. La hiedra asomaba
al muro del parque, negra y polvorienta...
La fuente sonaba.

Rechinó en la vieja cancela mi llave;
con agrio ruido abrióse la puerta
de hierro mohoso y, al cerrarse, grave
golpeó el silencio de la tarde muerta.

En el solitario parque, la sonora
copla borbollante del agua cantora
me guió a la fuente. La fuente vertía
sobre el blanco mármol su monotonía.

La fuente cantaba: ¿Te recuerda, hermano,
un sueño lejano mi canto presente?
Fue una tarde lenta del lento verano.

Respondí a la fuente:
No recuerdo, hermana,
mas sé que tu copla presente es lejana.

Fue esta misma tarde: mi cristal vertía
como hoy sobre el mármol su monotonía.
¿Recuerdas, hermano? ... Los mirtos talares,
que ves, sombreaban los claros cantares
que escuchas. Del rubio color de la llama,
el fruto maduro pendía en la rama,
lo mismo que ahora. ¿Recuerdas, hermano? ...
Fue esta misma lenta tarde de verano.

—No sé qué me dice tu copla riente
de ensueños lejanos, hermana la fuente.

A cold afternoon of winter,
gloomy. School children
study. Monotony
of rain on windows.

VI

It was a clear evening, a melancholy
dreamlike summer evening. The ivy appearing
on the walls of the park was black and dusty.
                    The fountain was singing.

My key rattled in the old iron grating;
with a harsh noise the heavy, rusty
iron door opened, and, then closing,
struck the silence of the dead evening.

In the deserted park, the bubbling
sonorous song of water singing
led me to the fountain spilling
over the white marble its monotony.

The fountain was singing: Does my chant remind you,
brother, of a distant dream?
It was a slow evening of slow summer.

I answered the question the fountain put to me:
Sister, I cannot say,
but I know your present song is far away.

It was this same evening: my crystal spilling
over the marble its monotony.
Do you remember, brother? . . . The spreading myrtle
was shading this very melody.
The ripened fruit in flaming colors
hung upon the boughs the same as now.
Do you remember, brother? . . .
It was that same slow evening of summer.

—I know not what your song is saying,
fountain sister, of distant dreams.

Yo sé que tu claro cristal de alegría
ya supo del árbol la fruta bermeja;
yo sé que es lejana la amargura mía
que sueña en la tarde de verano vieja.

Yo sé que tus bellos espejos cantores
copiaron antiguos delirios de amores:
mas cuéntame, fuente de lengua encantada,
cuéntame mi alegre leyenda olvidada.

Yo no sé leyendas de antigua alegría,
sino historias viejas de melancolía.

Fue una clara tarde del lento verano...
Tú venías solo con tu pena, hermano;
tus labios besaron mi linfa serena,
y en la clara tarde, dijeron tu pena.

Dijeron tu pena tus labios que ardían;
la sed que ahora tienen, entonces tenían.

—Adiós para siempre, la fuente sonora,
del parque dormido eterna cantora.
Adiós para siempre; tu monotonía,
fuente, es más amarga que la pena mía.

Rechinó en la vieja cancela mi llave;
con agrio ruido abrióse la puerta
de hierro mohoso y, al cerrarse, grave
sonó en el silencio de la tarde muerta.

VII

El limonero lánguido suspende
una pálida rama polvorienta
sobre el encanto de la fuente limpia,
y allá en el fondo sueñan
los frutos de oro...
                Es una tarde clara,
casi de primavera;
tibia tarde de marzo,
que el hálito de abril cercano lleva;

I know your glass of happiness
knew long ago the red fruit of the tree;
I know how distant is my old bitterness
that in the summer evening dreams.

I know your beautiful mirror's song
copied ancient raptures of love:
but tell me, fountain of enchanted tongue,
tell me my forgotten legend of joy.

—I do not know legends of ancient joys,
only histories, melancholy and old.

It was a clear evening of slow summer. . .
You came alone with your sorrow, brother;
your lips kissed my placid waters
and in the soft evening told your sorrow.

They told your sorrow, your lips that burned;
the thirst they now have, they had then.

—Goodbye forever, sonorous fountain,
eternal singer of the sleeping garden.
Goodbye forever, your monotony
is far more bitter than my grief.

My key rattled in the old iron grating;
with a harsh noise the heavy, rusty
iron door opened, and, then closing,
sounded in the silence of the dead evening.

VII

The languid lemon tree suspends
a branch, dusty and pale,
over the charm of the clear fountain,
and there in the depths
the golden fruits dream. . .
                    It is a clear evening,
nearly spring,
a warm March evening
that the breath of coming April brings;

y estoy solo, en el patio silencioso,
buscando una ilusión cándida y vieja:
alguna sombra sobre el blanco muro,
algún recuerdo, en el pretil de piedra
de la fuente dormido, o, en el aire,
algún vagar de túnica ligera.

En el ambiente de la tarde flota
ese aroma de ausencia
que dice al alma luminosa: nunca,
y al corazón: espera.

Ese aroma que evoca los fantasmas
de las fragancias vírgenes y muertas.

Sí, te recuerdo, tarde alegre y clara,
casi de primavera,
tarde sin flores, cuando me traías
el buen perfume de la hierbabuena,
y de la buena albahaca
que tenía mi madre en sus macetas.

Que tú me viste hundir mis manos puras
en el agua serena,
para alcanzar los frutos encantados
que hoy en el fondo de la fuente sueñan...

Sí, te conozco, tarde alegre y clara,
casi de primavera.

VIII

Yo escucho los cantos
de viejas cadencias
que los niños cantan
cuando en corro juegan,
y vierten en coro
sus almas que sueñan,
cual vierten sus aguas
las fuentes de piedra:
con monotonías

and in the still courtyard, I am alone,
seeking an illusion, innocent, old:
some shadow on the white wall,
some memory sleeping on the stone
of the fountain's edge, or, in the air,
the drifting of some diaphanous gown.

And in the evening atmosphere
that scent of absence floats,
which says to the luminous soul: never,
and to the heart: hope.

That scent which evokes the ghosts
of fragrances, virginal and dead.

Yes, I remember you, clear and joyous evening,
nearly spring,
the evening without flowers, when
you gave me sweet perfume of mint
and of sweet basil,
that my mother grew in pots of clay.

You saw me dip my white hands
into the waters serene,
to reach the enchanted fruits
that deep in the fountain dream. . .

Yes, I know you, clear and joyous evening,
nearly spring.

VIII

I listen to ballads
of ancient rhythms
that children are singing
in groups where they're playing,
and they spill forth in chorus
their souls that are dreaming,
as the fountains of marble
are spilling their waters
with the monotonous bubbling

de risas eternas
que no son alegres,
con lágrimas viejas
que no son amargas
y dicen tristezas,
tristezas de amores
de antiguas leyendas.

En los labios niños,
las canciones llevan
confusa la historia
y clara la pena;
como clara el agua
lleva su conseja
de viejos amores
que nunca se cuentan.

Jugando, a la sombra
de una plaza vieja,
los niños cantaban...

La fuente de piedra
vertía su eterno
cristal de leyenda.

Cantaban los niños
canciones ingenuas,
de un algo que pasa
y que nunca llega:
la historia confusa
y clara la pena.

Seguía su cuento
la fuente serena;
borrada la historia,
contaba la pena.

X

A la desierta plaza
conduce un laberinto de callejas.
A un lado, el viejo paredón sombrío

of laughter eternal
that is not truly joyful,
and tears that are ancient
but not truly bitter,
and tell of old sorrows,
the sorrows of loves
of long-ago legends.

On the lips of the children
the simple songs carry
a story obscure
with the pain very clear;
as the clear water
still carries its tales
of long-ago loves
that never are told.

Playing in the shade
of an ancient plaza,
the children were singing. . .

The fountain of marble
as always was spilling
its legend eternal.

The children were singing
those songs in their innocence
of something that passes and never gets here:
the story obscure
and the pain very clear.

The serene marble fountain
continued its tale;
with the story forgotten
it told of the pain.

X

To the deserted plaza
leads a labyrinth of streets.
On one side, the old shady wall

de una ruinosa iglesia;
a otro lado, la tapia blanquecina
de un huerto de cipreses y palmeras,
y, frente a mí, la casa,
y en la casa, la reja,
ante el cristal que levemente empaña
su figurilla plácida y risueña.
Me apartaré. No quiero
llamar a tu ventana. . . Primavera
viene—su veste blanca
flota en el aire de la plaza muerta—;
viene a encender las rosas
rojas de tus rosales. . . Quiero verla. . .

XVII *Horizonte*

En una tarde clara y amplia como el hastío,
cuando su lanza blande el tórrido verano,
copiaban el fantasma de un grave sueño mío
mil sombras en teoría, enhiestas sobre el llano.

La gloria del ocaso era un purpúreo espejo,
era un cristal de llamas, que al infinito viejo
iba arrojando el grave soñar en la llanura. . .
Y yo sentí la espuela sonora de mi paso
repercutir lejana en el sangriento ocaso,
y más allá, la alegre canción de un alba pura.

XVIII *El poeta*

Maldiciendo su destino
como Glauco, el dios marino,
mira, turbia la pupila
de llanto, el mar que le debe su blanca virgen Scyla.

El sabe que un Dios más fuerte
con la sustancia inmortal está jugando a la muerte,
cual niño bárbaro. El piensa

of a ruined church;
on the other, the white mud wall
around cypresses and palms;
in front of me the house,
and on the house the window
with its wrought-iron grating
blurring her smiling figure.
I draw away. I won't call
to your window. . . Spring comes
—its white gown floats
in the air of the dead plaza—;
it comes to light the red roses
of your bushes. . . I want to see her.

XVII *Horizon*

On an evening clear and large as weariness,
when the torrid summer brandishes its spear,
a thousand parading shadows, standing on a plain,
copied the ghost of my solemn dream.

The glory of the west was a purple mirror,
a flaming crystal flung to the infinite
by the solemn dreaming of the plains. . .
And the sharp crack of my footsteps I could hear
resounding far into the bleeding west,
and the joyous song of a pure dawn, beyond.

XVIII *The Poet*

Cursing his destiny
like the sea god Glaucus,
with his eye made cloudy by his weeping,
he stares at the sea that owes him his white virgin Scylla.

He knows that a stronger God
of immortal substance is playing with death,
like a barbarous child. He thinks

que ha de caer como rama que sobre las aguas flota,
antes de perderse, gota
de mar, en la mar inmensa.

En sueños oyó el acento de una palabra divina;
en sueños se le ha mostrado la cruda ley diamantina,
sin odio ni amor, y el frío
soplo del olvido sabe sobre un arenal de hastío.

Bajo las palmeras del oäsis el agua buena
miró brotar de la arena;
y se abrevó entre las dulces gacelas, y entre los fieros
animales carniceros...

Y supo cuánto es la vida hecha de sed y dolor.
Y fue compasivo para el ciervo y el cazador,
para el ladrón y el robado,
para el pájaro azorado,
para el sanguinario azor.

Con el amargo sabio dijo: Vanidad de vanidades,
todo es negra vanidad;
y oyó otra voz que clamaba, alma de sus soledades:
sólo eres tú, luz que fulges en el corazón, verdad.

Y viendo cómo lucían
miles de blancas estrellas,
pensaba que todas ellas
en su corazón ardían.

¡Noche de amor!
Y otra noche
sintió la mala tristeza
que enturbia la pura llama,
y el corazón que bosteza,
y el histrión que declama.

Y dijo: las galerías
del alma que espera están
desiertas, mudas, vacías:
las blancas sombras se van.

Y el demonio de los sueños abrió el jardín encantado
del ayer. ¡Cuán bello era!

that as a branch upon the water floats
before it disappears, so should a drop of sea
fall, into the immense sea.

    In dreams he heard the accent of a holy word;
in dreams appeared the law—unyielding, cruel,
of neither hate nor love,—and oblivion's
cold breath blows over the sandy ground of weariness.

    Beneath the oasis palms he watched
sweet water seeping from the sand;
and he drank of it, midst gentle gazelles
and flesh-eating beasts. . .

    And he learned how life is made of pain and thirst.
And he knew compassion for the hunter and the stag,
for the victim and the thief,
for the bird scared by the hawk,
and for the savage hawk.

    With the bitter sage he said: Vanity of vanities,
all is black vanity;
and he heard another voice that cried, the soul of his solitude:
there is only you, the light that blazes in the heart, truth.

    And when he saw the glowing
of thousands of white stars,
he thought that all were burning
deep within his heart.

Night of love!
                And another night
he felt the aching sadness
that clouds the perfect flame,
the weary heart that yawns,
the actor who declaims.

    And he said: The corridors
of the soul that hopes and waits
are deserted, empty, mute;
the white shadows go away.

    And the demon of his dreams opened the enchanted garden
of yesterday. How fair it was!

¡Qué hermosamente el pasado
fingía la primavera,
cuando del árbol de otoño estaba el fruto colgado,
mísero fruto podrido,
que en el hueco acibarado
guarda el gusano escondido!

¡Alma, que en vano quisiste ser más joven cada día,
arranca tu flor, la humilde flor de la melancolía!

XIX

¡Verdes jardinillos,
claras plazoletas,
fuente verdinosa
donde el agua sueña,
donde el agua muda
resbala en la piedra! . . .

Las hojas de un verde
mustio, casi negras,
de la acacia, el viento
de la septiembre besa,
y se lleva algunas
amarillas, secas,
jugando, entre el polvo
blanco de la tierra.

Linda doncellita
que el cántaro llenas
de agua transparente,
tú al verme, no llevas
a los negros bucles
de tu cabellera,
distraídamente,
la mano morena,
ni, luego, en el limpio
cristal te contemplas. . .

How beautifully the past
masqueraded as the spring,
when from the autumn tree hung the fruit,
that rotten fruit,
whose empty husk
holds the hidden worm!

Soul, who in vain desired to be younger,
uproot your humble flower, melancholy.

XIX

Green little gardens,
clear little plazas,
dark green fountain,
where the water is dreaming,
where the mute water
slips over the rock! . . .

The wind of September
is kissing the leaves
languid green, almost black
of the withering acacia,
and is carrying away
some of the leaves dry and yellow
that are playing in the white
dry dust of the earth.

Pretty little maiden
filling the pitcher
with transparent water,
upon noticing me
you no longer raise
—in that carefree way—
your dark hand to the curls
of your rich black hair,
or in the clean crystal
contemplate your reflection.

Tú miras al aire
de la tarde bella,
mientras de agua clara
el cántaro llenas.

You gaze at the air
of the beautiful evening,
while filling the pitcher
with the clear water.

DEL CAMINO
OF THE ROAD

XX *Preludio*

Mientras la sombra pasa de un santo amor, hoy quiero
poner un dulce salmo sobre mi viejo atril.
Acordaré las notas del órgano severo
al suspirar fragante del pífano de abril.

Madurarán su aroma las pomas otoñales,
la mirra y el incienso salmodiarán su olor;
exhalarán su fresco perfume los rosales,
bajo la paz en sombra del tibio huerto en flor.

Al grave acorde lento de música y aroma,
la sola y vieja y noble razón de mi rezar
levantará su vuelo suave de paloma,
y la palabra blanca se elevará al altar.

XXI

Daba el reloj las doce... y eran doce
golpes de azada en tierra...
... ¡Mi hora!—grité—. ... El silencio
me respondió: —No temas;
tú no verás caer la última gota
que en la clepsidra tiembla.

Dormirás muchas horas todavía
sobre la orilla vieja,
y encontrarás una mañana pura
amarrada tu barca a otra ribera.

XXII

Sobre la tierra amarga,
caminos tiene el sueño
laberínticos, sendas tortuosas,
parques en flor y en sombra y en silencio;

criptas hondas, escalas sobre estrellas;
retablos de esperanzas y recuerdos.

XX *Prelude*

While the shadow of a sacred love is passing,
I set a psalm on my music stand today;
and to the fragrant piping of the flute of April,
I shall tune the organ and begin to play.

The myrrh and incense will sing hymns of sweetness,
maturing apples will perfume the air;
the roses will exhale a scent of freshness
in the flowering shade of the peaceful orchard here.

To the solemn harmony of song and scent
the ancient noble purpose of my life
will send up a prayer on its soft dove flight:
and unto the altar the white word shall rise.

XXI

The clock struck twelve. . . twelve strokes
of the spade upon the earth. . .
. . . My time!—I cried—. . . .The quiet
answered: Do not fear;
the last drop in the water clock
you will not see fall.

You will sleep many hours yet
while still on the old shore;
then you'll find a pure tomorrow,
your boat on the other side moored.

XXII

Over the bitter land,
dreams have tortuous paths,
labyrinthine roads,
parks in flower, silence, shadow;

deep crypts, stairways over stars;
altarpieces of memories and hopes.

Figurillas que pasan y sonríen
—juguetes melancólicos de viejo—;

   imágenes amigas,
a la vuelta florida del sendero,
y quimeras rosadas
que hacen camino... lejos...

XXIV

   El sol es un globo de fuego,
la luna es disco morado.

   Una blanca paloma se posa
en el alto ciprés centenario.

   Los cuadros de mirtos parecen
de marchito velludo empolvado.

   ¡El jardín y la tarde tranquila!...
Suena el agua en la fuente de mármol.

XXV

   ¡Tenue rumor de túnicas que pasan
sobre la infértil tierra!...
¡Y lágrimas sonoras
de las campanas viejas!

   Las ascuas mortecinas
del horizonte humean...
Blancos fantasmas lares
van encendiendo estrellas.

   —Abre el balcón. La hora
de una ilusión se acerca...
La tarde se ha dormido
y las campanas sueñan.

Figurines that smile and pass
—melancholy toys of old—;

friendly images
at the flowering turn of the path,
and rose chimeras
that make their way... far...

XXIV

The sun is a globe of fire,
the moon a purple disk.

A white dove alights
on the century-old cypress.

The beds of myrtle seem
of withered, dusty velvet.

The garden and the tranquil evening! ...
The water sounds in the marble fountain.

XXV

Faint rustle of passing gowns
upon the sterile land! ...
And sonorous tears
from ancient bells!

The horizon's dying coals
still smoke.
White ghost gods
light up the stars.

—The balcony opens.
The hour of an illusion nears...
The evening has fallen asleep
and the bells dream.

XXVI

¡Oh, figuras del atrio, más humildes
cada día y lejanas:
mendigos harapientos
sobre marmóreas gradas;

miserables ungidos
de eternidades santas,
manos que surgen de los mantos viejos
y de las rotas capas!

¿Pasó por vuestro lado
una ilusión velada,
de la mañana luminosa y fría
en las horas más plácidas? . . .

Sobre la negra túnica, su mano
era una rosa blanca. . .

XXVIII

Crear fiestas de amores
en nuestro amor pensamos,
quemar nuevos aromas
en montes no pisados,

y guardar el secreto
de nuestros rostros pálidos,
porque en las bacanales de la vida
vacías nuestras copas conservamos,

mientras con eco de cristal y espuma
ríen los zumos de la vid dorados.
. . . .
Un pájaro escondido entre las ramas
del parque solitario,
silba burlón. . .
                    Nosotros exprimimos
la penumbra de un sueño en nuestro vaso. . .
Y algo, que es tierra en nuestra carne, siente
la humedad del jardín como un halago.

XXVI

Oh, figures of the atrium, distant
and more humble every day:
ragged beggars
on marble stairs;

miserable anointed priests
of sacred eternities,
hands that come forth
from the torn capes and old cloaks!

Did a veiled illusion
pass by your side
from the morning luminous and cold
in the calmest hours?

On the black tunic, the hand
was a white rose.

XXVIII

To make love festivals
in our love we plan,
to burn new fragrances
in mountains not trod upon,

and guard the secret
of our pallid faces,
for in life's bacchic banquets
we keep our glasses empty,

while in the echo of crystal and champagne
laugh the golden juices of the vine.
. . . .
A bird concealed among the branches
of the secluded park
whistles, mockingly. . .
                                    We press
the shadow of a dream into our glass. . .
and something that is earth within our flesh
feels the garden's moisture as a caress.

XXIX

Arde en tus ojos un misterio, virgen
esquiva y compañera.
No sé si es odio o es amor la lumbre
inagotable de tu aljaba negra.

Conmigo irás mientras proyecte sombra
mi cuerpo y quede a mi sandalia arena.
—¿Eres la sed o el agua en mi camino?
Dime, virgen esquiva y compañera.

XXXV

Al borde del sendero un día nos sentamos.
Ya nuestra vida es tiempo, y nuestra sola cuita
son las desesperantes posturas que tomamos
para aguardar... Mas Ella no faltará a la cita.

XXXVI

Es una forma juvenil que un día
a nuestra casa llega.
Nosotros le decimos: ¿por qué tornas
a la morada vieja?
Ella abre la ventana, y todo el campo
en luz y aroma entra.
En el blanco sendero,
los troncos de los árboles negrean;
las hojas de sus copas
son humo verde que a lo lejos sueña.
Parece una laguna
el ancho río entre la blanca niebla
de la mañana. Por los montes cárdenos
camina otra quimera.

XXIX

There burns a mystery in your eyes,
my elusive virgin companion.

I know not if it is hate or love,
your black quiver's eternal fire.

You will go with me while my body casts a shadow
and sand still clings to my sandal.

Are you thirst or water along my road?
Tell me, my elusive virgin companion.

XXXV

On the side of the path we sit down one day.
Now our life is time, and our only care
the positions we take in despair
to wait. But Death won't fail to appear.

XXXVI

At our house one day
there appears a youthful form.
We ask: why do you return
to your old abode?
It opens the window, and the whole field
enters in scent and light.
On the white path
the tree trunks grow black;
their leaves become green smoke
dreaming far away.
The wide river seems a lagoon
in the white morning haze.
In the livid mountains
another chimera walks.

XXXVII

¡Oh, dime, noche amiga, amada vieja,
que me traes el retablo de mis sueños
siempre desierto y desolado, y sólo
con mi fantasma dentro,
mi pobre sombra triste
sobre la estepa y bajo el sol de fuego,
o soñando amarguras
en las voces de todos los misterios,
dime, si sabes, vieja amada, dime
si son mías las lágrimas que vierto!
Me respondió la noche:
Jamás me revelaste tu secreto.
Yo nunca supe, amado,
si eras tú ese fantasma de tu sueño,
ni averigüé si era su voz la tuya,
o era la voz de un histrión grotesco.

Dije a la noche: Amada mentirosa,
tú sabes mi secreto;
tú has visto la honda gruta
donde fabrica su cristal mi sueño,
y sabes que mis lágrimas son mías,
y sabes mi dolor, mi dolor viejo.

¡Oh! Yo no sé, dijo la noche, amado,
yo no sé tu secreto,
aunque he visto vagar ese, que dices
desolado fantasma, por tu sueño.
Yo me asomo a las almas cuando lloran
y escucho su hondo rezo,
humilde y solitario,
ese que llamas salmo verdadero;
pero en las hondas bóvedas del alma
no sé si el llanto es una voz o un eco.

Para escuchar tu queja de tus labios
yo te busqué en tu sueño,
y allí te vi vagando en un borroso
laberinto de espejos.

XXXVII

Oh tell me, friendly night, my old beloved,
who brings my stage of dreams,
forever desolate, deserted,
and only my ghost within,
my poor sad shadow
on the barren plain under the fiery sun,
or dreaming bitterness
in the voices of all the mysteries,
tell me if you know, old beloved, tell me
if the tears I spill are mine!
The night replied:
you never revealed your secret to me.
Beloved, I never knew
if you were that ghost of your dream,
nor did I learn if its voice was yours
or that of an actor grotesque.

I said to the night: Beloved liar,
you know my secret;
you have seen the cavern
where my dream makes its glass,
and you know that my tears are mine
and you know my ancient pain.

Oh beloved, said the night, I do not know,
I do not know your secret,
though I have seen your desolate ghost
(as you say) wandering through your dream.
I appear to souls when they are crying,
and I listen to their deep prayers,
solitary and humble,
what you would call the true psalm;
but in the deep vaults of the soul
I know not if the weeping is voice or echo.

To hear the plaint of your lips
I sought you in your dream,
and there in a blurred labyrinth of mirrors
I saw you wandering.

CANCIONES
SONGS

XXXVIII

Abril florecía
frente a mi ventana.
Entre los jazmines
y las rosas blancas
de un balcón florido,
vi las dos hermanas.
La menor cosía,
la mayor hilaba...
Entre los jazmines
y las rosas blancas,
la más pequeñita,
risueña y rosada
—su aguja en el aire—,
miró a mi ventana.

La mayor seguía,
silenciosa y pálida,
el huso en su rueca
que el lino enroscaba.
Abril florecía
frente a mi ventana.

Una clara tarde
la mayor lloraba,
entre los jazmines
y las rosas blancas,
y ante el blanco lino
que en su rueca hilaba.
—¿Qué tienes—le dije—
silenciosa pálida?
Señaló el vestido
que empezó la hermana.
En la negra túnica
la aguja brillaba;
sobre el velo blanco,
el dedal de plata.
Señaló a la tarde
de abril que soñaba,
mientras que se oía

XXXVIII

April was flowering
in front of my window.
Among all the jasmine
and the white roses
of a flowering balcony,
I saw the two sisters.
The younger was sewing,
the older was spinning.
Among all the jasmine
and the white roses,
the one who was smaller,
rosy and smiling
—her needle in the air—,
gazed at my window.

The one who was older,
so pale and so silent,
kept the spinning wheel turning
that twisted the linen.
April was flowering
in front of my window.

One clear evening,
the older was weeping,
among all the jasmine
and the white roses,
before the white linen
that she was spinning.
What is wrong—I asked her—
pale, silent one?
She pointed to the dress
that her sister had begun.
Against the black gown
the needle shone;
upon the white veil
the thimble of silver. . .
She pointed to the dreaming
evening of April,
while the sound of bells ringing

ta ñer de campanas.
Y en la clara tarde
me enseñó sus lágrimas...
Abril florecía
frente a mi ventana.
    Fue otro abril alegre
y otra tarde plácida.
El balcón florido
solitario estaba...
Ni la pequeñita
risueña y rosada,
ni la hermana triste,
silenciosa y pálida,
ni la negra túnica,
ni la toca blanca...
Tan sólo en el huso
el lino giraba
por mano invisible,
y en la oscura sala
la luna del limpio
espejo brillaba...
Entre los jazmines
y las rosas blancas
del balcón florido,
me miré en la clara
luna del espejo
que lejos soñaba...
Abril florecía
frente a mi ventana.

XL *Inventario galante*

    Tus ojos me recuerdan
las noches de verano,
negras noches sin luna,
orilla al mar salado,
y el chispear de estrellas
del cielo negro y bajo.

far away could be heard.
And in the clear evening
she showed me her tears. . .
April was flowering
in front of my window.

It was another happy April
and another placid evening.
The flowering balcony
was empty. . .
Neither the smaller sister
rosy and smiling,
nor the sad sister,
pale and silent,
nor the white bonnet,
nor the black gown. . .
Only on the spindle
the linen was turning
by an invisible hand,
and through the dark parlor
in the clean mirror
the moon was shining. . .
Among all the jasmine
and the white roses
of the flowering balcony,
I gazed at myself
in the clear moon of the mirror
that was distantly dreaming. . .
April was flowering
in front of my window.

XL *Gallant Inventory*

Your eyes remind me
of summer nights,
black nights that are moonless,
against the shores of the sea,
and the stars sparkling
in the low black sky.

Tus ojos me recuerdan
las noches de verano.
Y tu morena carne,
los trigos requemados,
y el suspirar de fuego
de los maduros campos.

Tu hermana es clara y débil
como los juncos lánguidos,
como los sauces tristes,
como los linos glaucos.
Tu hermana es un lucero
en el azul lejano. . .
Y es alba y aura fría
sobre los pobres álamos
que en las orillas tiemblan
del río humilde y manso.
Tu hermana es un lucero
en el azul lejano.

De tu morena gracia,
de tu soñar gitano,
de tu mirar de sombra
quiero llenar mi vaso.
Me embriagaré una noche
de cielo negro y bajo,
para cantar contigo,
orilla al mar salado,
una canción que deje
cenizas en los labios. . .
De tu mirar de sombra
quiero llenar mi vaso.

Para tu linda hermana
arrancaré los ramos
de florecillas nuevas
a los almendros blancos,
en un tranquilo y triste
alborear de marzo.
Los regaré con agua
de los arroyos claros,

Your eyes remind me
of summer nights.
And your dark flesh,
the sunburnt wheat,
and the fiery breath
of the ripened fields.

Your sister is fair and fragile,
like the languid rushes,
like the sad willows,
like the pale green flax.
Your sister is a morning star
in the distant blue. . .
And is dawn and cold breezes
over the poor poplar trees,
that on the shores shiver
by the gently flowing river.
Your sister is a morning star
in the distant blue.

Of your dark grace,
of your gypsy dreaming,
of your gaze of shadow
I want to fill my glass.
I shall get drunk on a night
of a low black sky,
to sing with you
on the shores of the sea,
a song that will leave
ashes on your lips.
Of your gaze of shadow
I want to fill my glass.

For your pretty sister
I shall tear off the boughs
newly covered with blossoms
from the white almond trees,
some early March morning,
tranquil and sad.
I shall sprinkle them with water
from the clear stream,

los ataré con verdes
junquillos del remanso...
Para tu linda hermana
yo haré un ramito blanco.

XLII

La vida hoy tiene ritmo
de ondas que pasan,
de olitas temblorosas
que fluyen y se alcanzan.

La vida hoy tiene el ritmo de los ríos,
la risa de las aguas
que entre los verdes junquerales corren,
y entre las verdes cañas.

Sueño florido lleva el manso viento;
bulle la savia joven en las nuevas ramas;
tiemblan alas y frondas,
y la mirada sagital del águila
no encuentra presa... treme el campo en sueños,
vibra el sol como un arpa.

¡Fugitiva ilusión de ojos guerreros,
que por las selvas pasas
a la hora del cenit: tiemble en mi pecho
el oro de tu aljaba!

En tus labios florece la alegría
de los campos en flor; tu veste alada
aroman las primeras velloritas,
las violetas perfuman tus sandalias.

Yo he seguido tus pasos en el viejo bosque,
arrebatados tras la corza rápida,
y los ágiles músculos rosados
de tus piernas silvestres entre verdes ramas.

¡Pasajera ilusión de ojos guerreros
que por las selvas pasas

tie them with green rushes
that grow in the river.
For your pretty sister,
I shall make a white bouquet.

XLII

Life today has the rhythm
of waves that are passing
and tremulous ripples
ebbing and flowing.

Life today has the rhythm of rivers,
the laughter of waters
that run through green reeds
and through the green rushes.

The softest breeze brings the flowery dream,
stirs the young sap in the new branches;
the wings and leaves are flickering;
the eagle's gaze does not find prey.
In dream, the meadow is trembling,
and like a harp the sun is vibrating.

Fleeting illusion of warrior's eyes,
at the zenith hour through the forest you pass;
and the gold you carry in your quiver
is trembling deep within my breast.

There blossoms on your lips the joy
of fields in bloom, while violets
perfume your sandals, the first cowslips
make sweet your dress.

In the ancient forest I've followed your steps
in their reckless chase of the deer,
and among green branches I have seen
your strong flushed legs, running free.

Fleeting illusion of warrior's eyes,
passing swiftly through the trees

cuando la tierra reverdece y ríen
los ríos en las cañas!
¡Tiemble en mi pecho el oro
que llevas en tu aljaba!

XLIII

Era una mañana y abril sonreía.
Frente al horizonte dorado moría
la luna, muy blanca y opaca; tras ella,
cual tenue ligera quimera, corría
la nube que apenas enturbia una estrella.
. . . .
Como sonreía la rosa mañana,
al sol del Oriente abrí mi ventana;
y en mi triste alcoba penetró el Oriente
en canto de alondras, en risa de fuente
y en suave perfume de flora temprana.

Fue una clara tarde de melancolía.
Abril sonreía. Yo abrí las ventanas
de mi casa al viento... El viento traía
perfumes de rosas, doblar de campanas...

Doblar de campanas lejanas, llorosas,
suave de rosas aromado aliento...
...¿Dónde están los huertos floridos de rosas?
¿Qué dicen las dulces campanas al viento?
. . . .
Pregunté a la tarde de abril que moría:
¿Al fin la alegría se acerca a mi casa?
La tarde de abril sonrió: La alegría
pasó por tu puerta—y luego, sombría:
Pasó por tu puerta. Dos veces no pasa.

XLIV

El casco roído y verdoso
del viejo falucho
reposa en la arena...

when the ground grows green again
and the rivers laugh in the reeds!

The gold you carry in your quiver
is trembling deep within my breast.

XLIII

It was a spring morning and April was smiling.
On the other side of the sky from this golden horizon,
the moon, very white and opaque, now was dying;
behind her like a faint, translucent chimera
the cloud that barely hides stars now was fleeing.
. . . .

As the bright rosy morning of April was smiling,
to the sun in the east I opened my window;
and the east then entered into my sad chamber
in the singing of larks, in the laughter of fountains,
and in the soft perfume of the early flowers.

It was a clear melancholy spring evening.
April was smiling. I opened the windows
of my house to the wind, the wind which was bringing
the perfume of roses, the sound of bells ringing.

The ringing of bells, that cry in the distance,
the gentle breath of soft-smelling roses. . .
What do the sweet bells say to the wind?
Where are the flowering gardens of roses?
. . . .

I asked the dying April evening:
Is joy approaching my house this time?
The April evening smiled and replied:
Joy passed through your door—and then gloom.
It does not pass twice.

XLIV

The green corroded hull
of the old sloop
reposes in the sand. . .

La vela tronchada parece
que aún sueña en el sol y en el mar.

El mar hierve y canta...
El mar es un sueño sonoro
bajo el sol de abril.

El mar hierve y ríe
con olas azules y espumas de leche y de plata,
el mar hierve y ríe
bajo el cielo azul.

El mar lactescente,
el mar rutilante,
que ríe en sus liras de plata sus risas azules...
¡Hierve y ríe el mar!...

El aire parece que duerme encantado
en la fúlgida niebla de sol blanquecino.
La gaviota palpita en el aire dormido, y al lento
volar soñoliento, se aleja y se pierde en la bruma del sol.

The broken sail still seems
to dream in the sun and the sea.

The sea boils and sings.
The sea is a sonorous dream
under the April sun.

The sea boils and laughs
in blue waves and foam of milk and silver,
the sea boils and laughs
under the blue sky.

The milky sea,
the sparkling sea,
laughing its blue laughs in its silver lyres. . .
The sea boils and laughs.

The air seems to dream,
enchanted in the white sun's bright mist.
The sea gull quivers in the sleeping air
and in a slow dreaming flight into the sun's haze disappears.

GALERÍAS
GALLERIES

LXI *Introducción*

Leyendo un claro día
mis bien amados versos,
he visto en el profundo
espejo de mis sueños

que una verdad divina
temblando está de miedo,
y es una flor que quiere
echar su aroma al viento.

El alma del poeta
se orienta hacia el misterio.
Sólo el poeta puede
mirar lo que está lejos
dentro del alma, en turbio
y mago sol envuelto.

En esas galerías,
sin fondo, del recuerdo,
donde las pobres gentes
colgaron cual trofeo

el traje de una fiesta
apolillado y viejo,
allí el poeta sabe
el laborar eterno
mirar de las doradas
abejas de los sueños.

Poetas, con el alma
atenta al hondo cielo,
en la cruel batalla
o en el tranquilo huerto,

la nueva miel labramos
con los dolores viejos,
la veste blanca y pura
pacientemente hacemos,
y bajo el sol bruñimos
el fuerte arnés de hierro.

LXI *Introduction*

Reading one clear day
my well loved lines,
I saw in the deep
mirror of my dreams

that a divine truth
lies quivering with fear,
a flower that wants
to send its scent to the wind.

The soul of the poet
turns towards the mystery.
Only the poet can see
what lies in the cloudy depths
of the soul
hidden in magic sun.

In those bottomless galleries
of the memory
where poor people
hung like a trophy

the dress of a festival
moth-eaten and old,
there the poet knows
the eternal labor
of the golden bees
of his dreams.

Poets, with the soul
attentive to the deepest sky,
in the cruel battle
or in the orchard in peace,

produce the new honey
with ancient pains,
patiently make
the pure white gown,
and polish the iron harness
in the burning sun.

El alma que no sueña,
el enemigo espejo,
proyecta nuestra imagen
con un perfil grotesco.

Sentimos una ola
de sangre, en nuestro pecho,
que pasa... y sonreímos,
y a laborar volvemos.

LXIII

Y era el demonio de mi sueño, el ángel
más hermoso. Brillaban
como aceros los ojos victoriosos,
y las sangrientas llamas
de su antorcha alumbraron
la honda cripta del alma.

—¿Vendrás conmigo? —No, jamás; las tumbas
y los muertos me espantan.
Pero la férrea mano
mi diestra atenazaba.

—Vendrás conmigo... Y avancé en mi sueño,
cegado por la roja luminaria.
Y en la cripta sentí sonar cadenas
y rebullir de fieras enjauladas.

LXIV

Desde el umbral de un sueño me llamaron...
Era la buena voz, la voz querida.

Dime; ¿vendrás conmigo a ver el alma?...
Llegó a mi corazón una caricia.

—Contigo siempre... Y avancé en mi sueño
por una larga, escueta galería,
sintiendo el roce de la veste pura
y el palpitar suave de la mano amiga.

The soul that won't dream,
the enemy mirror,
projects our image
as a grotesque form.

In our breast we feel
a wave of blood
that passes. . . we smile
and return to work.

LXIII

And it was the demon of my dreams,
the most beautiful angel. His victorious eyes
like bright steel shone,
and the bloody flames
of his torch brought light
to the deep crypt of the soul.

—Will you come with me?—No, never;
the tombs and the dead make me afraid.
But his hand of iron
was gripping mine.

—You shall come with me. . . And blinded by the red glare
I advanced in my dream.
And in the crypt I heard the rattling of chains
and the stirring of caged beasts.

LXIV

They called me from the threshold of a dream. . .
It was the good voice, the beloved voice.

—Tell me, will you come with me to see the soul? . . .
My heart sensed a caress.

—With you always. . . And through a long empty gallery
in my dream I advanced,
feeling the swish of the pure gown
and the gentle pulse of the friendly hand.

LXVIII

Llamó a mi corazón, un claro día,
con un perfume de jazmín, el viento.
—A cambio de este aroma,
todo el aroma de tus rosas quiero.
—No tengo rosas; flores
en mi jardín no hay ya: todos han muerto.
Me llevaré los llantos de las fuentes,
las hojas amarillas y los mustios pétalos.
Y el viento huyó... Mi corazón sangraba...
Alma, ¿qué has hecho de tu pobre huerto?

LXX

Y nada importa ya que el vino de oro
rebose de tu copa cristalina,
o el agrio zumo enturbie el puro vaso...

Tú sabes las secretas galerías
del alma, los caminos de los sueños,
y la tarde tranquila
donde van a morir... Allí te aguardan

las hadas silenciosas de la vida,
y hacia un jardín de eterna primavera
te llevarán un día.

LXXI

¡Tocados de otros días,
mustios encajes y marchitas sedas;
salterios arrumbados,
rincones de las salas polvorientas;

daguerrotipos turbios,
cartas que amarillean;
libracos no leídos
que guardan grises florecitas secas:

LXVIII

One clear day, with the perfume of jasmine,
the wind called to my heart.

—In return for this scent,
the scent of your roses I want.
—I have no roses; in my garden
are no more flowers: all died.

I shall carry away the weeping of fountains,
the yellowed leaves and the withered petals.
And the wind fled... My heart bled...
Soul, what have you done with your orchard?

LXX

And it matters not that the golden wine
from your crystal goblet overflows,
or that the bitter juices cloud the clear glass...

You know the secret galleries
of the soul, the roads of dreams,
and the tranquil evening
where they will die... The silent fairies

of life await you there,
and will carry you one day
to a garden of eternal spring.

LXXI

Coiffures of other days,
wrinkled silks and languid lace,
psalters hidden away,
corners of dusty drawing rooms;

distorted daguerreotypes;
yellowing letters;
unread worthless books
that hold gray dried flowers:

romanticismos muertos,
cursilerías viejas,
cosas de ayer que sois el alma, y cantos
y cuentos de la abuela!...

LXXV

Yo, como Anacreonte,
quiero cantar, reír y echar al viento
las sabias amarguras
y los graves consejos,

y quiero, sobre todo, emborracharme,
ya lo sabéis... ¡Grotesco!
Pura fe en el morir, pobre alegriá
y macabro danzar antes de tiempo.

LXXVIII

¿Y ha de morir contigo el mundo mago
donde guarda el recuerdo
los hálitos más puros de la vida,
la blanca sombra del amor primero,

la voz que fue a tu corazón, la mano
que tú querías retener en sueños,
y todos los amores
que llegaron al alma, al hondo cielo?

¿Y ha de morir contigo el mundo tuyo,
la vieja vida en orden tuyo y nuevo?
¿Los yunques y crisoles de tu alma
trabajan para el polvo y para el viento?

LXXIX

Desnuda está la tierra,
y el alma aúlla al horizonte pálido
como loba famélica. ¿Qué buscas,
poeta, en el ocaso?

dead romanticisms,
old vulgarities,
things of yesterday that are the soul,
and songs and tales of the grandmother! . . .

LXXV

I, like Anacreon,
want to sing, laugh, and throw to the wind
the wise bitterness
and the grave advice,

and want, above all, to get drunk,
now you know. . . Grotesque!
Sheer faith in the dying, poor joy
and macabre dancing before time.

LXXVIII

And will it die with you, the magic world
where memory holds
the purest breaths of life,
the white shadow of the first love,

the hand you longed to keep in dreams,
the voice that went to your heart and mind,
and all the loves
that reached the soul and the deepest sky?

And will it die with you, your whole world,
age-old life in the new form that is your own?
Are the anvils and crucibles of your soul
working for the dust and for the wind?

LXXIX

Naked is the land,
and at the pale horizon the soul
howls like a famished wolf.
What do you seek in the sunset, poet?

¡Amargo caminar, porque el camino
pesa en el corazón! ¡El viento helado,
y la noche que llega, y la amargura
de la distancia! . . . En el camino blanco

algunos yertos árboles negrean;
en los montes lejanos
hay oro y sangre. . . El sol murió. . . ¿Qué buscas,
poeta, en el ocaso?

LXXXII *Los sueños*

El hada más hermosa ha sonreído
al ver la lumbre de una estrella pálida
que en hilo suave, blanco y silencioso,
se enrosca al huso de su rubia hermana.

Y vuelve a sonreír, porque en su rueca
el hilo de los campos se enmaraña.
Tras la tenue cortina de la alcoba
está el jardín envuelto en luz dorada.

La cuna, casi en sombra. El niño duerme.
Dos hadas laboriosas lo acompañan,
hilando de los sueños los sutiles
copos en ruecas de marfil y plata.

LXXXVIII

Tal vez la mano, en sueños,
del sembrador de estrellas,
hizo sonar la música olvidada

como una nota de la lira inmensa,
y la ola humilde a nuestros labios vino
de unas pocas palabras verdaderas.

A bitter walk, for the road
weighs heavy on the heart. The icy wind
and the coming night, and the bitterness
of the distance! On the white road

some rigid trees grow black;
there is blood and gold
on the mountains far away. . . The sun has died.
What do you seek in the sunset, poet?

LXXXII *Dreams*

The most beautiful fairy smiles
on seeing the pale light of a star
twist around the spindle of her fair sister
in thread soft and silent and white.

On her distaff—she smiles—
is the thread of the fields entwined.
Behind the flimsy bedroom curtain
the garden is golden in light.

The cradle, in shadow. The child asleep.
Two fairies attend him,
and on distaffs of ivory and silver
spin the slender bundles from his dreams.

LXXXVIII

Perhaps, in dreams, the hand
of the sower of the stars
made the forgotten music sound

as a note from the great lyre,
and to our lips came the humble wave
of a few true words.

LXXXIX

Y podrás conocerte recordando
del pasado soñar los turbios lienzos,
en este día triste en que caminas
con los ojos abiertos.

De toda la memoria, sólo vale
el don preclaro de evocar los sueños.

LXXXIX

And you shall know when you recall
the cloudy canvasses you used to dream
on this sad day when you walk
with open eyes.

Of all that is in your memory, only the gift
of evoking dreams is worth anything.

VARIA
MISCELLANEOUS

XCIII

Deletreos de armonía
que ensaya inexperta mano.

Hastío. Cacofonía
del sempiterno piano
que yo de niño escuchaba
soñando... no sé con qué,

con algo que no llegaba,
todo lo que ya se fue.

XCIII

The spelling out of harmony
by an inexpert hand.

Weariness. Cacophony
of the everlasting piano
which I listened to as a child,
while dreaming... of what I do not know,

of something that would not arrive,
all that had already gone.

CAMPOS DE CASTILLA
LAND OF CASTILE

XCIX *Por tierras de España*

El hombre de estos campos que incendia los pinares
y su despojo aguarda como botín de guerra,
antaño hubo raído los negros encinares,
talado los robustos robledos de la sierra.

Hoy ve sus pobres hijos huyendo de sus lares;
la tempestad llevarse los limos de la tierra
por los sagrados ríos hacia los anchos mares;
y en páramos malditos trabaja, sufre y yerra.

Es hijo de una estirpe de rudos caminantes,
pastores que conducen sus hordas de merinos
a Extremadura fértil, rebaños trashumantes
que mancha el polvo y dora el sol de los caminos.

Pequeño, ágil, sufrido, los ojos de hombre astuto,
hundidos, recelosos, movibles; y trazadas
cual arco de ballesta, en el semblante enjuto
de pómulos salientes, las cejas muy pobladas.

Abunda el hombre malo del campo y de la aldea,
capaz de insanos vicios y crímenes bestiales,
que bajo el pardo sayo esconde un alma fea,
esclava de los siete pecados capitales.

Los ojos siempre turbios de envidia o de tristeza,
guarda su presa y llora la que el vecino alcanza;
ni para su infortunio ni goza su riqueza;
le hieren y acongojan fortuna y malandanza.

El numen de estos campos es sanguinario y fiero:
al declinar la tarde, sobre el remoto alcor,
veréis agigantarse la forma de un arquero,
la forma de un inmenso cantauro flechador.

Veréis llanuras bélicas y páramos de asceta
—no fue por estos campos el bíblico jardín—;
son tierras para el águila, un trozo de planeta
por donde cruza errante la sombra de Caín.

XCIX *Across the Land of Spain*

The man of this country who burns the pine
and waits for his plunder as spoils of war
long ago razed the black oak groves,
laid waste the great oaks of the mountain woods.

He sees his sons flee their dwellings today,
the storm take away the soil of the earth
through the sacred rivers to the wide seas;
on cursed plateaus, he suffers, works.

He belongs to a line of rugged wanderers,
shepherds who lead their nomadic hordes
to Extremadura, the flocks of sheep
that the dust stains dark and the sun turns gold.

Long-enduring, cunning, small;
high cheekbones, deep distrustful eyes
that dart from under heavy brows
drawn on that face like a crossbow's arch.

The bad man of the country and of the village is here,
with his insane vices and bestial crimes,
who in his brown cloak hides an ugly soul,
who is slave to the seven deadly sins.

His eyes ever cloudy with envy or sorrow,
he guards his own prey and covets his neighbor's,
neither fights his poverty nor enjoys his wealth;
he grieves for both fortune and misery.

The god of these lands is bloodthirsty, cruel:
as the afternoon fades over the distant knoll,
you will see the form of an archer loom,
the form of a giant centaur with bow.

You will see plains for warriors, plateaus for hermits
—the biblical garden was not of this land—;
this is country for the eagle, a piece of planet
where crosses the wandering shadow of Cain.

C *El hospicio*

Es el hospicio, el viejo hospicio provinciano,
el caserón ruinoso de ennegrecidas tejas
en donde los vencejos anidan en verano
y graznan en las noches de invierno las cornejas.

Con su frontón al Norte, entre los dos torreones
de antigua fortaleza, el sórdido edificio
de grietados muros y sucios paredones,
es un rincón de sombra eterna. ¡El viejo hospicio!

Mientras el sol de enero su débil luz envía,
su triste luz velada sobre los campos yermos,
a un ventanuco asoman, al declinar el día,
algunos rostros pálidos, atónitos y enfermos,

a contemplar los montes azules de la sierra;
o, de los cielos blancos, como sobre una fosa,
caer la blanca nieve sobre la fría tierra,
¡sobre la tierra fría la nieve silenciosa! . . .

CI *El Dios ibero*

Igual que el ballestero
tahúr de la cantiga,
tuviera una saeta el hombre ibero
para el Señor que apedreó la espiga
y malogró los frutos otoñales,
y un "gloria a ti" para el Señor que grana
centenos y trigales
que el pan bendito le darán mañana.

"Señor de la ruina,
adoro porque aguardo y porque temo:
con mi oración se inclina
hacia la tierra un corazón blasfemo.

"Señor, por quien arranco el pan con pena,
sé tu poder, conozco mi cadena!
¡Oh, dueño de la nube del estío

C *The Asylum*

It is the asylum, the old asylum of the province,
the great ruined house of blackened tiles
where the swifts nest in the summertime
and the crows caw on the winter nights.

Between two ancient fortress towers
its gable faces north; the building,
squalid with cracked and dirty walls,
is a corner of eternal shadow. The asylum!

While the January sun sends its feeble light,
its sad veiled light on the barren fields,
as the day declines, at a miserable window
pallid faces, sick and bewildered, appear,

to contemplate the blue peaks of the mountains;
or, from the white skies, as if over a grave,
the falling of the white snow on the cold land,
the silent snow on the cold landscape! . . .

CI *The Iberian God*

Like the archer in the ballad—
the gambler of the song—,
the Iberian man sent an arrow
to the Lord who stoned his wheat
and killed the fall fruits with hail,
and a "Glory to Thee" to the Lord
who sows his fields of grain
which will bring him the blessed bread.

"Lord of the ruin,
I worship in hope and fear:
with my prayer a blasphemous heart
bows to the earth here.

"Lord, by whom I seize my bread with pain,
I know thy power, I recognize my chain!
Oh master of the summer cloud

que la campiña arrasa,
del seco otoño, del helar tardío,
y del bochorno que la mies abrasa!

"¡Señor del iris sobre el campo verde
donde la oveja pace,
Señor del fruto que el gusano muerde
y de la choza que el turbión deshace,

"tu soplo el fuego del hogar aviva,
tu lumbre da sazón al rubio grano,
y cuaja el hueso de la verde oliva,
la noche de San Juan, tu santa mano!

"¡Oh dueño de fortuna y de pobreza,
ventura y malandanza,
que al rico das favores y pereza
y al pobre su fatiga y su esperanza!

"¡Señor, Señor: en la voltaria rueda
del año he visto mi simiente echada,
corriendo igual albur que la moneda
del jugador en el azar sembrada!

"¡Señor, hoy paternal, ayer cruento,
con doble faz de amor y de venganza,
a Ti, en un dado de tahúr al viento
va mi oración, blasfemia y alabanza!"

Este que insulta a Dios en los altares,
no más atento al ceño del destino,
también soñó caminos en los mares
y dijo: es Dios sobre el mar camino.

¿No es él quien puso a Dios sobre la guerra,
más allá de la suerte,
más allá de la tierra,
más allá de la mar y de la muerte?

¿No dio la encina ibera
para el fuego de Dios la buena rama,
que fue en la santa hoguera
de amor una con Dios en pura llama?

that flattens the land,
of the dry autumn and the late freeze,
and of the scorching heat that burns the grain!

"Lord of the rainbow, over the green fields
where the sheep graze,
Lord of the fruit that the worm eats
and the hovel that the storm takes,

"thy breath quickens the fire in the hearth,
thy light ripens the golden grain;
on the night of St. John thy holy hand
brings forth the green olive seed.

"Oh master of fortune and poverty,
of misery and joy,
who gives favors and idleness to the rich,
hope and weariness to the poor!

"Lord, Lord: I have seen my seed
tossed on the year's capricious wheel,
running the same risk as the gambler's coin
that is at random thrown.

"Lord, paternal today, yesterday cruel,
with the double face of love and revenge,
to thee, in a gambler's gift to the wind,
goes my prayer of blasphemy and praise."

This man who hurls insults to God from the altars,
no longer attentive to destiny's frown,
has also dreamed roads upon the sea
and said: the road on the sea is God.

Is it not he who put God above war,
beyond earth,
beyond chance,
beyond sea and death?

Did not the Iberian oak
give its branch for the fire of God,
merging with God in flame
in the holy blaze of love?

Mas hoy. . . ¡Qué importa un día!
Para los nuevos lares
estepas hay en la floresta umbría,
leña verde en los viejos encinares.

Aún larga patria espera
abrir al corvo arado sus besanas;
para el grano de Dios hay sementera
bajo cardos y abrojos y bardanas.

¡Qué importa un día! Está el ayer alerto
al mañana, mañana al infinito,
hombres de España; ni el pasado ha muerto,
ni está el mañana—ni el ayer—escrito.

¿Quién ha visto la faz al Dios hispano?
Mi corazón aguarda
al hombre ibero de la recia mano,
que tallará en el roble castellano
el Dios adusto de la tierra parda.

CVI *Un loco*

Es una tarde mustia y desabrida
de un otoño sin frutos, en la tierra
estéril y raída
donde la sombra de un centauro yerra.

Por un camino en la árida llanura,
entre álamos marchitos,
a solas con su sombra y su locura,
va el loco, hablando a gritos.

Lejos se ven sombríos estepares,
colinas con malezas y cambrones,
y ruinas de viejos encinares,
coronando los agrios serrijones.

El loco vocifera
a solas con su sombra y su quimera.
Es horrible y grotesca su figura;

But today . . . what does a day matter!
For the new hearths
there are plains in the shady woods,
green firewood in the old oak groves.

The large fatherland is waiting still
to open its furrows to the bent plow;
beneath burdocks, thorns, and thistle,
there is land to be sown for the grain of God.

What does a day matter! Yesterday is alert
to the morrow, tomorrow to the infinite;
men of Spain, the past is not dead,
and tomorrow and yesterday are not written.

Who has seen the face of the Spanish God?
My heart awaits
the Iberian man of the strong hand
who will carve on the Castilian oak
the austere God of the brown land.

CVI *A Madman*

It is a bleak and dismal evening
of a fruitless autumn, on the worn out
sterile land
where a centaur's shadow wanders.

Among the withered poplar trees,
along a road on the barren plain,
alone with his shadow and his madness
goes the madman, howling.

Far away one sees dark fields of rockrose,
hills grown over with weeds and brambles,
and ruins of old oaks
crowning the jagged mountains.

The madman cries out
with his shadow and his chimera alone.
His body is horrible, grotesque,

flaco, sucio, maltrecho y mal rapado,
ojos de calentura
iluman su rostro demacrado.
Huye de la ciudad... Pobres maldades,
misérrimas virtudes y quehaceres
de chulos aburridos y ruindades
de ociosos mercaderes.

Por los campos de Dios el loco avanza.
Tras la tierra esquelética y sequiza
—rojo de herrumbre y pardo de ceniza—
hay un sueño de lirio en lontananza.

Huye de la ciudad. ¡El tedio urbano!
—¡carne triste y espíritu villano!—

No fue por una trágica amargura
esta alma errante desgajada y rota;
purga un pecado ajeno: la cordura,
la terrible cordura del idiota.

CXV *A un olmo seco*

Al olmo viejo, hendido por el rayo
y en su mitad podrido,
con las lluvias de abril y el sol de mayo,
algunas hojas verdes le han salido.

¡El olmo centenario en la colina
que lame el Duero! Un musgo amarillento
le mancha la corteza blanquecina
al tronco carcomido y polvoriento.

No será, cual los álamos cantores
que guardan el camino y la ribera,
habitado de pardos ruiseñores.

Ejército de hormigas en hilera
va trepando por él, y en sus entrañas
urden sus telas grises las arañas.

bony, battered, dirty, unshaved;
feverish eyes
illuminate his wasted face.

He flees the city. . . Poor vices,
shabby affairs, miserable virtues
of bored and tiresome crooks
and idle merchants.

The madman advances through the fields of God.
Beyond the parched and naked land
—red from rust and brown from ash—
in the distance is a lily dream.

He flees the city. The urban ennui.
—rude spirit, abject flesh!—

It was not a tragic bitterness
made this wandering soul, ragged, sundered;
he atones for another's sin: the sanity,
the terrible sanity of the idiot.

CXV *To a Withered Elm*

On an old elm, rotten in its center
and by a bolt of lightning split,
with the rains of April and the sun of May,
some green leaves have appeared.

The century-old elm on the hill
that the waters of the Duero touch!
A moss stains yellow the whitish bark
of the worm-eaten, dusty trunk.

Unlike the singing poplar trees
that guard the road and the bank,
it won't house brown nightingales.

In single file an army of ants
bores through it, and in its entrails
the spiders weave their gray web.

Antes que te derribe, olmo del Duero,
con su hacha el leñador, y el carpintero
te convierta en melena de campana,
lanza de carro o yugo de carreta;
antes que rojo en el hogar, mañana,
ardas de alguna mísera caseta,
el borde de un camino;
antes que te descuaje un torbellino
y tronche el soplo de las sierras blancas;
antes que el río hasta la mar te empuje
por valles y barrancas,
olmo, quiero anotar en mi cartera
la gracia de tu rama verdecita.
Mi corazón espera
también, hacia la luz y hacia la vida,
otro milagro de la primavera.

CXXII

Soñé que tú me llevabas
por una blanca vereda,
en medio del campo verde,
hacia el azul de las sierras,
hacia los montes azules,
una mañana serena.

Sentí tu mano en la mía,
tu mano de compañera,
tu voz de niña en mi oído
como una campana nueva,
como una campana virgen
de un alba de primavera.
¡Eran tu voz y tu mano,
en sueños, tan verdaderas! . . .
Vive, esperanza, ¡quién sabe
lo que se traga la tierra!

Before the woodsman chops you down,
old elm on the Duero, and the carpenter
puts you to use in a bell tower,
or as a wagon axle or yoke;
before red in the fireplace, tomorrow,
you lie burning in some miserable hut
standing by the side of the road;
before a whirlwind uproots you
and the mountain blast breaks you;
before the river pushes you to the sea
through valleys and ravines,
old elm, I want to note
the grace of your leafy limb.
My heart too looks in hope
towards light and life
for another miracle of spring.

CXXII

I dreamed you were taking me
on a path of white flowers
across wide green fields
toward the blue mountains
toward the blue of the peaks
one peaceful morning.

In my hand I felt your hand,
the hand of my companion,
and in my ear your young voice
like a new bell ringing
like a virgin bell in the springtime
in the dawn of the morning.
Your voice and your hand
were so real in my dreaming! . . .
Stay alive, hope, who knows
what the earth will swallow!

CXXIII

Una noche de verano
—estaba abierto el balcón
y la puerta de mi casa—
la muerte en mi casa entró.
Se fue acercando a su lecho
—ni siquiera me miró—,
con unos dedos muy finos
algo muy tenue rompió.
Silenciosa y sin mirarme,
la muerte otra vez pasó
delante de mí. ¿Qué has hecho?
La muerte no respondió.
Mi niña quedó tranquila,
dolido mi corazón.
¡Ay, lo que la muerte ha roto
era un hilo entre los dos!

CXXVI *A José María Palacio*

Palacio, buen amigo,
¿está la primavera
vistiendo ya las ramas de los chopos
del río y los caminos? En la estepa
del alto Duero, primavera tarda,
¡pero es tan bella y dulce cuando llega! . . .
¿Tienen los viejos olmos
algunas hojas nuevas?
Aún las acacias estarán desnudas
y nevados los montes de las sierras.
¡Oh, mole del Moncayo blanca y rosa,
allá, en el cielo de Aragón, tan bella!
¿Hay zarzas florecidas
entre las grises peñas,
y blancas margaritas
entre la fina hierba?
Por esos campanarios
ya habrán ido llegando las cigüeñas.

CXXIII

One summer night
—the door of my house
and my balcony were open—
death entered my house.
Without glancing at me
it approached my bed,
and with very fine fingers
broke something frail.
Silent, without glancing at me
death passed by again.
What have you done?
Death did not respond.
My little girl was still,
my heart in pain.
Oh, what death broke
was a thread
between us.

CXXVI *To José María Palacio*

Palacio, good friend,
has the spring come again,
clothing the poplar branch
of the river and the roads? On the barren plain
of the high Duero, spring arrives late,
but when she arrives is beautiful and sweet! . . .
Do the old elms have new leaves?
The acacia will still be bare,
and snow will cover the mountain peaks.
Oh, huge Moncayo white and pink,
beautiful against the sky of Aragon!
Do blackberry bushes blossom
among the gray stones,
and white daisies
in the young grass?
To those belfries
the storks will have come.

Habrá trigales verdes,
y mulas pardas en las sementeras,
y labriegos que siembran los tardíos
con las lluvias de abril. Ya las abejas
libarán del tomillo y el romero.
¿Hay ciruelos en flor? ¿Quedan violetas?
Furtivos cazadores, los reclamos
de la perdiz bajo las capas luengas,
no faltarán. Palacio, buen amigo,
¿tienen ya ruiseñores las riberas?
Con los primeros lirios
y las primeras rosas de las huertas,
en una tarde azul, sube al Espino,
al alto Espino donde está su tierra. . .

CXXXVI *Proverbios y cantares*

I

Nunca perseguí la gloria
ni dejar en la memoria
de los hombres mi canción;
yo amo los mundos sutiles,
ingrávidos y gentiles
como pompas de jabón.
Me gusta verlos pintarse
de sol y grana, volar
bajo el cielo azul, temblar
súbitamente y quebrarse.

XXIX

Caminante, son tus huellas
el camino, y nada más;
caminante, no hay camino,
se hace camino al andar.
Al andar se hace camino,
y al volver la vista atrás
se ve la senda que nunca
se ha de volver a pisar.

There will be green rows of wheat,
and brown mules in newly planted fields,
and farmers sowing late
with the April rains. Even now the bees
sip from rosemary and thyme.
Are there plum trees in bloom? Do violets remain?
There will be no lack of sly hunters
with partridge lures under long capes.
Palacio, good friend,
have nightingales come to the river banks?
With the first lilies
and the first roses of the gardens,
go up to the Espino on a blue afternoon,
the high Espino which is her land. . .

CXXXVI *Proverbs and Songs*

I

Never did I pursue glory
or try to leave my song
in the memory of men;
I love the subtle worlds,
graceful and weightless
as bubbles of soap.
I like to see them, painted
in sun and red grain,
fly beneath the blue sky,
tremble suddenly and break.

XXIX

Wanderer, your footsteps are
the road, and nothing more;
wanderer, there is no road,
the road is made by walking.
By walking one makes the road,
and upon glancing behind
one sees the path
that never will be trod again.

Caminante, no hay camino,
sino estelas en la mar.

XXXV

Hay dos modos de conciencia;
una es luz, y otra, paciencia.
Una estriba en alumbrar
un poquito el hondo mar;
otra, en hacer penitencia
con caña o red, y esperar
el pez, como pescador.
Dime tú: ¿Cuál es mejor?
¿Conciencia de visionario
que mira en el hondo acuario
peces vivos,
fugitivos,
que no se pueden pescar,
o esa maldita faena
de ir arrojando a la arena,
muertos, los peces del mar?

XLV

Morir. . . ¿Caer como gota
de mar en el mar inmenso?
¿O ser lo que nunca he sido:
uno, sin sombra y sin sueño,
un solitario que avanza
sin camino y sin espejo?

LIII

Ya hay un español que quiere
vivir y a vivir empieza,
entre una España que muere
y otra España que bosteza.
Españolito que vienes
al mundo, te guarde Dios.
Una de las dos Españas
ha de helarte el corazón.

Wanderer, there is no road—
only wakes upon the sea.

XXXV

There are two modes of consciousness:
one is light; the other, patience.
One lies in illuminating
a little the sea's depths;
the other in doing penance
with a fishing pole or net,
and, like a fisherman, waiting for the fish.
Which is better? Tell me.
The consciousness of the visionary
gazing into the deep aquarium
at live fish,
fugitives,
that cannot be caught,
or that cursed task
of flinging onto the sand
the fish of the sea—dead.

XLV

To die. . . To fall as a drop
of sea into the immense sea?
Or to be what I have never been:
a man without shadow and without dream,
a solitary man advancing
without road and without mirror.

LIII

Now there is a Spaniard
who wants to live and begins to live,
between one Spain that dies
and another Spain that yawns.
May God keep you, little Spaniard
that to the world is born.
One of these Spains
will freeze your heart.

CXXXVIII *Mi bufón*

El demonio de mis sueños
ríe con sus labios rojos,
sus negros y vivos ojos,
sus dientes finos, pequeños.
Y jovial y picaresco
se lanza a un baile grotesco,
luciendo el cuerpo deforme
y su enorme
joroba. Es feo y barbudo,
y chiquitín y panzudo.
Yo no sé por qué razón,
de mi tragedia, bufón,
te ríes... Mas tú eres vivo
por tu danzar sin motivo.

CXXXVIII *My Buffoon*

The demon of my dreams
with his red lips is laughing,
with his eyes black and flashing,
his fine, little teeth.
And jovial and picaresque
he flings himself into a dance grotesque,
showing off his deformed body
and his ugly
enormous hump. He is bearded,
repulsive, tiny, big-bellied.
Buffoon, I don't know why
you laugh at my tragedy.
But you are a lively one
to dance without reason.

NUEVAS CANCIONES
NEW SONGS

CLVI *Galerías*

I

En el azul la banda
de unos pájaros negros
que chillan, aletean y se posan
en el álamo yerto.
. . . En el desnudo álamo,
las graves chovas quietas y en silencio,
cual negras, frías notas
escritas en la pauta de febrero.

II

El monte azul, el río, las erectas
varas cobrizas de los finos álamos,
y el blanco del almendro en la colina,
¡oh nieve en flor y mariposa en árbol!
Con el aroma del habar, el viento
corre en la alegre soledad del campo.

III

Una centella blanca
en la nube de plomo culebrea.
¡Los asombrados ojos
del niño, y juntas cejas
—está el salón oscuro—de la madre! . . .
¡Oh cerrado balcón a la tormenta!
El viento aborrascado y el granizo
en el limpio cristal repiquetean.

IV

El iris y el balcón.
             Las siete cuerdas
de la lira del sol vibran en sueños.
Un tímpano infantil da siete golpes
—agua y cristal—.
             Acacias con jilgueros.
Cigüeñas en las torres.
             En la plaza,
lavó la lluvia el mirto polvoriento.

CLVI *Galleries*

I

In the blue a flock
of cawing black birds,
flapping their wings, perched
on the rigid poplar tree.
. . . In the bare poplar tree,
somber, silent crows,
like cold, black notes
written on the staff of February.

II

The blue peaks, the river, the straight
copper-colored twigs of the poplars,
and the almond tree white on the hill,
oh, snow on flower, butterfly on tree!
With fragrance of beanfields, the wind
blows through the happy solitude of the land.

III

White lightning
snakes through the leaden cloud.
The startled eyes
of the child, and in the dark room
the furrowed brows of the mother! . . .
Balcony closed to the storm!
The tempestuous wind and the hail
beat the clean glass.

IV

The iris and the balcony.
                          The seven chords
of the sun's lyre quiver in dreams.
A child's drum gives seven beats
—glass and water—.
                          Linnets in the acacia.
Storks in the towers.
                          In the plaza
the rain has washed the dusty myrtle.

En el amplio rectángulo ¿quién puso
ese grupo de vírgenes risueño,
y arriba ¡hosanna! entre la rota nube,
la palma de oro y el azul sereno?

V

Entre montes de almagre y peñas grises,
el tren devora su raíl de acero.
La hilera de brillantes ventanillas
lleva un doble perfil de camafeo,
tras el cristal de plata, repetido...
¿Quién ha punzado el corazón del tiempo?

VI

¿Quién puso, entre las rocas de ceniza,
para la miel del sueño,
esas retamas de oro
y esas azules flores del romero?
La sierra de violeta
Y, en el poniente, el azafrán del cielo,
¿quién ha pintado? ¡El abejar, la ermita,
el tajo sobre el río, el sempiterno
rodar del agua entre las hondas peñas,
y el rubio verde de los campos nuevos,
y todo, hasta la tierra blanca y rosa
al pie de los almendros!

VII

En el silencio sigue
la liga pitagórica vibrando,
el iris en la luz, la luz que llena
mi estereoscopio vano.
Han cegado mis ojos las cenizas
del fuego heraclitano.
El mundo es, un momento,
transparente, vacío, ciego, alado.

In the wide square, who placed
that group of smiling virgins,
and above—hosannah!—in the torn cloud,
the golden palm and the peaceful blue?

V

Through mountains of red earth and gray cliffs,
the train devours its steel rail.
In the double shining windows
are rows of cameo profiles,
behind the silver panes, again and again. . .
Who has pierced the heart of time?

VI

Who placed among the ashen boulders,
for the honey of dreams,
the blue flowers of rosemary
and that furze of gold?
The purple mountains
and, in the West, the saffron sky,
who painted it? The beehive,
the hermitage, the river's cliffs,
the water rolling endlessly between great rocks,
and the light green of new fields,
all of it, even the earth white and pink
at the foot of the almond trees!

VII

In the silence
the Pythagorean lyre sounds,
the rainbow in the light, the light
in my useless stereoscope.
The ashes of the Heraclitean fire
have blinded my eyes.
The world is, for a moment,
transparent, blind, empty, winged.

CLXI *Proverbios y cantares*

A JOSÉ ORTEGA Y GASSET

I

El ojo que ves no es
ojo porque tú lo veas;
es ojo porque te ve.

VIII

Hoy es siempre todavía.

XXXVI

No es el yo fundamental
eso que busca el poeta,
sino el tú esencial.

LXIV

¿Conoces los invisibles
hiladores de los sueños?
Son dos: la verde esperanza
y el torvo miedo.

Apuesta tienen de quien
hile más y más ligero,
ella, su copo dorado;
él, su copo negro.

Con el hilo que nos dan
tejemos, cuando tejemos.

XCIII

¿Cuál es la verdad? ¿El río
que fluye y pasa
donde el barco y el barquero
son también ondas del agua?
¿O este soñar del marino
siempre con ribera y ancla?

XCIX

—¿Mas el arte?—

—Es puro juego,

CLXI *Proverbs and Songs*
TO JOSÉ ORTEGA Y GASSET

I
The eye that you see is not
an eye because you see it;
it is an eye because it sees you.

VIII
Today is always yet.

XXXVI
It is not the fundamental I
that the poet seeks,
but the essential you.

LXIV
Do you know the invisible
spinners of dreams?
There are two: green hope
and grim fear.

They have a bet on the one
who can faster spin:
she, her spool of gold,
he, his spool of black.

With the thread they give
we weave, when we weave.

XCIII
What is truth? The river
that flows and passes
where the boat and the boatsman
are also waves of the water?
Or this dreaming of the sailor
always of shore and anchor?

XCIX
—But art? . . .
              It is pure game,

que es igual a pura vida,
que es igual a puro fuego.
Veréis el ascua encendida.

CLXII *Parergón: Los ojos*

AL GIGANTE IBÉRICO, MIGUEL DE UNAMUNO, POR QUIEN
LA ESPAÑA ACTUAL ALCANZA PROCERIDAD EN EL MUNDO.

I

Cuando murió su amada
pensó en hacerse viejo
en la mansión cerrada,
solo, con su memoria y el espejo
donde ella se miraba un claro día.
Como el oro en el arca del avaro,
pensó que guardaría
todo un ayer en el espejo claro.
Ya el tiempo para él no correría.

II

Mas pasado el primer aniversario,
¿cómo eran—preguntó—, pardos o negros,
sus ojos? ¿Glaucos? . . . ¿Grises?
¿Cómo eran, ¡Santo Dios!, que no recuerdo? . . .

III

Salió a la calle un día
de primavera, y paseó en silencio
su doble luto, el corazón cerrado. . .
De una ventana en el sombrío hueco
vio unos ojos brillar. Bajó los suyos,
y siguió su camino. . . ¡Como ésos!

CLXIV *Glosando a Ronsard y otras rimas*

ESTO SOÑÉ

Que el caminante es suma del camino,
y en el jardín, junto del mar sereno,

that is like pure life,
that is like pure fire.
You shall see the burning ember.

CLXII *Ornament: The Eyes*

TO THE IBERIAN GIANT, MIGUEL DE UNAMUNO, BY WHOM
SPAIN ACHIEVES DISTINCTION IN THE WORLD.

I
When his beloved died
he decided to grow old
secluded in the mansion
with his memory, alone,
with the mirror where she had gazed at herself.
And he thought that he would hold
in the clear mirror all of yesterday
as the coffer holds the miser's gold.
Time for him would no longer pass.

II
But when the first year had gone by,
how were her eyes, pale green or gray?
or black or brown? Oh God!
I don't recall—how were they?

III
He went out into the street one day
of spring, and silently in double mourning
walked about with his heart closed.
At a window in the shadows above
he saw some eyes shine. He lowered his own,
and continued walking. . . Like those!

CLXIV *Variations on Ronsard and Other Rhymes*

THIS I DREAMED
That the wanderer is sum of the road,
and in the garden, next to the peaceful sea,

le acompaña el aroma montesino,
ardor de seco henil en campo ameno;

que de luenga jornada peregrino
ponía al corazón un duro freno,
para aguardar el verso adamantino
que maduraba el alma en su hondo seno.

Esto soñé. Y del tiempo, el homicida,
que nos lleva a la muerte o fluye en vano,
que era un sueño no más del adanida.

Y un hombre vi que en la desnuda mano
mostraba al mundo el ascua de la vida,
sin cenizas el fuego heraclitano.

DE MI CARTERA

I   Ni mármol duro y eterno,
ni música ni pintura,
sino palabra en el tiempo.

II   Canto y cuento es la poesía.
Se canta una viva historia,
contando su melodía.

III   Crea el alma sus riberas;
montes de ceniza y plomo,
sotillos de primavera.

IV   Toda la imaginería
que no ha brotado del río,
barata bisutería.

V   Prefiere la rima pobre,
la asonancia indefinida.
Cuando nada cuenta el canto,
acaso huelga la rima.

VI   Verso libre, verso libre. . .
Líbrate, mejor, del verso
cuando te esclavice.

the mountain air accompanies him,
the heat of dry hay in the halcyon fields;

that as a pilgrim on a long journey
he held his heart in check
to await the adamantine verses
his soul nurtured in his breast.

I dreamed of this. And of the killer time,
that carries us to death or flows in vain,
no more than a dream of Adam, paradise.

And I saw a man who in his bare hand
showed to the world the burning embers of life,
the fire of Heraclitus without ash.

FROM MY BRIEFCASE

I Neither marble, hard and eternal,
nor painting nor music,
but the word in time.

II Song and tale is poetry.
One sings a living history,
telling its melody.

III The soul creates its banks,
mountains of ash and lead,
little groves of spring.

IV All the imagery
that has not come forth from the river,
cheap jewelry.

V Prefer the poor rhyme,
assonance undefined.
When the song tells nothing
perhaps there is idle rhyme.

VI Free verse, free verse. . .
Better, free yourself from the verse
when it enslaves you.

VII   La rima verbal y pobre,
y temporal, es la rica.
El adjetivo y el nombre,
remansos del agua limpia,
son accidentes del verbo
en la gramática lírica,
del Hoy que será Mañana,
del Ayer que es Todavía.

VII   The verbal, poor, and temporal rhyme
        is the rich rhyme.
        The adjective and the noun,
        backwater of the pure water,
        are accidents of the verb
        in the lyric grammar,
        of Today that will be Tomorrow,
        and the Yesterday that is Yet.

DE UN CANCIONERO APÓCRIFO

FROM AN APOCRYPHAL SONGBOOK

ROSA DE FUEGO
Tejidos sois de primavera, amantes,
de tierra y agua y viento y sol tejidos.
La sierra en vuestros pechos jadeantes,
en los ojos los campos florecidos,

pasead vuestra mutua primavera,
y aun bebed sin temor la dulce leche
que os brinda hoy la lúbrica pantera,
antes que, torva, en el camino aceche.

Caminad, cuando el eje del planeta
se vence hacia el solsticio de verano,
verde el almendro y mustia la violeta,

cerca la sed y el hontanar cercano,
hacia la tarde del amor, completa,
con la rosa de fuego en vuestra mano.

GUERRA DE AMOR
El tiempo que la barba me platea,
cavó mis ojos y agrandó mi frente,
va siendo en mí recuerdo transparente,
y mientras más al fondo, más clarea.

Miedo infantil, amor de adolescente,
¡cuánto esta luz de otoño os hermosea!,
¡agrios caminos de la vida fea,
que también os doráis al sol poniente!

¡Cómo en la fuente donde el agua mora
resalta en piedra una leyenda escrita:
al ábaco del tiempo falta un hora!

¡Y cómo aquella ausencia en una cita,
bajo las olmas que noviembre dora,
del fondo de mi historia resucita!

from CONSEJOS, COPLAS, APUNTES
La plaza tiene una torre,
la torre tiene un balcón,

CLXVII

ROSE OF FIRE

Woven you are of the springtime, lovers,
of water, earth, the sun and the winds.
In your heaving breasts the mountain,
in your eyes the flowering fields,

pass through the springtime you have together,
even drink without fear the sweet milk today
that is offered to you by the slippery panther,
before the fierce beast on the road lies in wait.

Walk on and on, when the axis of the planet
toward the solstice of summer is inclined,
green the almond, and languid the violet,

with thirst upon you, and the springs near by,
toward the evening of love, completed,
with the rose of fire in your hand.

WAR OF LOVE

Time that turns my beard to silver,
made wide my forehead, deep my eyes,
is becoming in me a transparent memory;
the deeper it goes, the more it brings to light.

Childhood fear, adolescent love,
you are beautiful in this autumn light!,
bitter roads of ugly life,
that at sunset also seem gold and bright.

In the fountain where the water lies
how clearly a legend is written in stone:
One hour less in the abacus of time!

And how that absence at an appointment long ago
from the depths of my history revives,
beneath the elms that November turns gold.

from ADVICE, VERSES, NOTES

The plaza has a tower,
the tower a balcony,

el balcón tiene una dama,
la dama, una blanca flor.
Ha pasado un caballero
—¡quién sabe por qué pasó!—,
y se ha llevado la plaza,
con su torre y su balcón,
con su balcón y su dama,
su dama y su blanca flor.

AL GRAN CERO

Cuando *el Ser que se es* hizo la nada
y reposó, que bien lo merecía,
ya tuvo el día noche, y compañía
tuvo el hombre en la ausencia de la amada.

Fiat umbra! Brotó el pensar humano.
Y el huevo universal alzó, vacío,
ya sin color, desustanciado y frío,
lleno de niebla ingrávida, en su mano.

Toma el cero integral, la hueca esfera,
que has de mirar, si lo has de ver, erguido.
Hoy que es espalda el lomo de tu fiera,

y es el milagro del no ser cumplido,
brinda, poeta, un canto de frontera
a la muerte, al silencio y al olvido.

CLXIX *Ultimas lamentaciones de Abel Martín*

Hoy, con la primavera,
soñé que un fino cuerpo me seguía
cual dócil sombra. Era
mi cuerpo juvenil, el que subía
de tres en tres peldaños la escalera.

—Hola, galgo de ayer. (Su luz de acuario
trocaba el hondo espejo
por agria luz sobre un rincón de osario.)
—Tú conmigo, rapaz?
                                    —Contigo, viejo.

the balcony a lady,
the lady a white flower.
A gentleman has passed,
—who knows why he passed!—
and he carried away the plaza
with its tower and its balcony,
with its balcony and its lady,
its lady and white flower.

TO THE GREAT ZERO

When the *Being Who Is* made nothingness,
and rested, for so he deserved,
then the day had night and darkness,
and man company in the absence of his love.

Fiat umbra! Human consciousness was born.
And the universal egg rose, and was known to man,
who held it, empty, cold, forlorn,
full of weightless mist, in his hand.

Take the integral zero, the hollow sphere,
and face it, standing tall, that it be in your vision.
Because the wild beast's back has become your shoulder,

and because it is the miracle of being without completion,
offer up today, poet, a song from the frontier
to death, to silence, and to oblivion.

CLXIX *Last Lament of Abel Martín*

With the springtime today,
I dreamed a delicate body was following me
as a gentle shadow. It was
my body, in childhood, that climbed
the stairs, three by three.

—Hello, young hound of yesterday. The aquarium
light was altered by the mirror
into the harsh light of an ossarium.
—You, are you with me, boy?
                    —With you, old man.

Soñé la galería
al huerto de ciprés y limonero;
tibias palomas en la piedra fría,
en el cielo de añil rojo pandero,
y en la mágica angustia de la infancia
la vigilia del ángel más austero.

La ausencia y la distancia
volví a soñar con túnicas de aurora;
firme en el arco tenso la saeta
del mañana, la vista aterradora
de la llama prendida en la espoleta
de su granada.
        ¡Oh Tiempo, oh Todavía
preñado de inminencias!
Tú me acompañas en la senda fría,
tejedor de esperanzas e impaciencias.

          *

¡El tiempo y sus banderas desplegadas!
(¿Yo, capitán? Mas yo no voy contigo.)
¡Hacia lejanas torres soleadas
el perdurable asalto por castigo!

          *

Hoy, como un día, en la ancha mar violeta
hunde el sueño su pétrea escalinata,
y hace camino la infantil goleta,
y le salta el delfín de bronce y plata.

La hazaña y la aventura
cercando un corazón entelerido. . .
Montes de piedra dura
—eco y eco—mi voz han repetido.

¡Oh, descansar en el azul del día
como descansa el águila en el viento,
sobre la sierra fría,
segura de sus alas y su aliento!

La augusta confianza
a ti, Naturaleza, y paz te pido,
mi tregua de temor y de esperanza,
un grano de alegría, un mar de olvido. . .

I dreamed the corridor
to the orchard of cypress and lemon trees;
warm doves on cold stone,
red kite in sky of indigo,
and the vigil of the most austere angel
in the magic anguish of infancy.

The absence and the distance
in robes of dawn again I dreamed;
the arrow of tomorrow firm
in the taut bow, the frightening vision
of the flame caught on the fuse
of its pomegranate.
                              Oh Time, yet
pregnant, imminent!
You accompany me on the cold path,
weaver of frustration and hope.

                    *

Time and its banners unfurled!
(I, captain? But I do not go with you.)
Toward distant sunlit towers,
in atonement, the everlasting assault!

                    *

Today, as one day, in the wide, violet sea,
the stony landing sinks into the dream,
the child's schooner goes its way,
and the bronze and silver dolphin leaps.

The adventure and the deed
enclosing a frightened heart. . .
Mountains of hard rock
—echoing—repeat my voice.

Oh, to rest in the blue of day
as the eagle rests in the wind,
over the cold ridge
sure of his breath and wings!

Nature, I ask of you
noble faith and peace,
my respite from hope and fear,
a grain of joy, a sea of oblivion.

CLXX *En memoria de Abel Martín*

Mientras traza su curva el pez de fuego,
junto al ciprés, bajo el supremo añil,
y vuela en blanca piedra el niño ciego,
en el olmo la copla de marfil
de la verde cigarra late y suena,
honremos al Señor
—la negra estampa de su mano buena—
que ha dictado el silencio en el clamor.
Al Dios de la distancia y de la ausencia,
del áncora en el mar, la plena mar. . .
El nos libra del mundo—omipresencia—,
nos abre senda para caminar.
Con la copa de sombra bien colmada,
con este nunca lleno corazón,
honremos al Señor que hizo la Nada
y ha esculpido en la fe nuestra razón.

CLXXII *Recuerdos de sueño, fiebre y duermivela*

I

Esta maldita fiebre
que todo me lo enreda,
siempre diciendo: ¡claro!
Dormido estás: despierta.
¡Masón, masón!
                Las torres
bailando están en rueda.
Los gorriones pían
bajo la lluvia fresca.
¡Oh, claro, claro, claro!
Dormir es cosa vieja,
y el toro de la noche
bufando está a la puerta.
A tu ventana llego
con una rosa nueva,
con una estrella roja
y la garganta seca.

CLXX *In Memory of Abel Martín*

While the fish of fire traces an arc,
by the cypress, through the deepest blue,
and the blind child flies in white stone,
and the green cricket's song of ivory hue
is sounding in the elm,
let us honor the Lord
—the black stamp of his good hand—
who spoke silence into the voices' storm.
To the God of distance and absence,
of the anchor in the sea, the wide sea. . .
He frees us from the world—omnipresence—,
opens for us a way.
With the goblet filled to the brim with shadow,
with this never full heart,
let us honor the Lord who made Nothingness
and in our faith our reason carved.

CLXXII *Memories from Dream, Fever, and Fitful Sleep*

I

This cursed fever
that holds me in its net,
is always saying: it's clear!
You are asleep: awake.
Mason, Mason!
The towers
are dancing in a round.
The sparrows are chirping
in the fresh rain.
Oh, it's clear, it's clear!
Sleeping is old,
and the bull of the night
is bellowing at the door.
At your window I arrive
with a new rose,
with a red star
and a dry throat.

¡Oh, claro, claro, claro!
¿Velones? En Lucena.
¿Cuál de las tres? Son una
Lucía, Inés, Carmela,
y el limonero baila
con la encinilla negra.
¡Oh, claro, claro, claro!
Dormido estás. Alerta.
Mili, mili, en el viento:
glu-glú, glu-glú, en la arena.
Los tímpanos del alba,
¡qué bien repiquetean!
¡Oh, claro, claro, claro!

II
En la desnuda tierra...

III
Era la tierra desnuda,
y un frío viento, de cara,
con nieve menuda.

Me eché a caminar
por un encinar de sombra:
la sombra de un encinar.

El sol las nubes rompía
con sus trompetas de plata.
La nieve ya no caía.

La vi un momento asomar
en las torres del olvido.
Quise y no pude gritar.

IV
¡Oh, claro, claro, claro!
Ya están los centinelas
alertos. ¡Y esta fiebre
que todo me lo enreda! ...
Pero a un hidalgo no
se ahorca; se degüella,

Oh, it's clear, it's clear!
Lamps? In Lucena.
Which of the three?Lucía, Inés, Carmela are
    one.
And the lemon tree dances
with the black oak.
Oh, it's clear, it's clear!
You are asleep. On guard!
Whistle, whistle, in the wind;
gurgle, gurgle, in the sand.
The dreams of the dawn,
how they peal!
Oh, it's clear, it's clear!

II
On the naked land. . .

III
It was the naked land,
and an oncoming cold wind,
with little snow.

I began to walk
through a shady oak grove:
the shadow of an oak.

The sun broke the clouds
with its silver trumpets.
The snow fell no more.

One moment I saw her appear
in the towers of oblivion.
I tried to scream but could not.

IV
Oh, it's clear, it's clear!
The sentinels are alerted now.
And this fever that holds
me totally in its net! . . .
But they do not hang
a nobleman; him they behead,

seor verdugo. ¿Duermes?
Masón, masón, despierta.
Nudillos infantiles
y voces de muñecas.

*

¡Tan-tan! ¿Quién llama, di?
—¿Se ahorca a un inocente
en esta casa?
                                    —Aquí
se ahorca, simplemente.

*

¡Qué vozarrón! Remacha
el clavo en la madera.
Con esta fiebre... ¡Chito!
Ya hay público a la puerta.
La solución más linda
del último problema.
Vayan pasando, pasen;
que nadie quede afuera.

*

¡Sambenitado, a un lado!
—¿Eso será por mí?
¿Soy yo el sambenitado,
señor verdugo?
                                    —Sí.

*

¡Oh, claro, claro, claro!
Se da trato de cuerda,
que es lo infantil, y el trompo
de música resuena.
Pero la guillotina,
una mañana fresca...
Mejor el palo seco,
y su corbata hecha.
¿Guitarras? No se estilan.
Fagotes y cornetas,
y el gallo de la aurora,
si quiere. ¿La reventa
la hacen los curas? ¡Claro!
¡¡¡Sambenitón, despierta!!!

sir hangman. Are you asleep?
Mason, mason, awake.
Babies' hands
and voices of dolls.

*

Tap-tap! Who calls? Speak!
—In this house do they hang
an innocent man?
                        —Here
they simply hang.

*

What a gruff voice! It pounds
the nail into the wood.
With this fever. . . Hush!
Somebody is already at the door.
The prettiest solution
to the last problem.
Come on in, come in;
may nobody stay outside.

*

Penitent, to the side!
—That will be for me?
Mr. Hangman, am I
the penitent?
                        —Yes.

*

Oh, it's clear, it's clear!
One is given the chord,
which is the infantile part,
and the musical top resounds.
But the guillotine
one cool morning. . .
Better the bare pole,
and the tie tied.
Guitars? They are not in style.
Bugles, bassoons,
and the cock at dawn,
if desired. Do the priests
do the sales? Clearly!
Old penitent, awake!

V

Con esta bendita fiebre
la luna empieza a tocar
su pandereta; y danzar
quiere, a la luna, la liebre.
De encinar en encinar
saltan la alondra y el día.
En la mañana serena
hay un latir de jauría,
que por los montes resuena.
Duerme. ¡Alegría! ¡Alegría!

VI

Junto al agua fría,
en la senda clara,
sombra dará algún día
ese arbolillo en que nadie repara.
Un fuste blanco y cuatro verdes hojas
que, por abril, le cuelga primavera,
y arrastra el viento de noviembre, rojas.
Su fruto, sólo un niño lo mordiera.
Su flor, nadie la vio. ¿Cuándo florece?
Ese arbolillo crece
no más que para el ave de una cita,
que es alma—campo y plumas—de un instante,
un pajarillo azul y petulante
que a la hora de la tarde lo visita.

VII

¡Qué fácil es volar, qué fácil es!
Todo consiste en no dejar que el suelo
se acerque a nuestros pies.
Valiente hazaña, ¡el vuelo!, ¡el vuelo!, ¡el vuelo!

VIII

¡Volar sin alas donde todo es cielo!
Anota este jocundo
pensamiento: Parar, parar el mundo
entre las puntas de los pies,

V

With this blessed fever
the moon starts to play
its tambourine; and the hare
wants to dance to the moon.
From grove to grove
spring the lark and the day.
A howling pack of hounds
in the morning serene
through the mountain resounds.
Sleep. Joy! Joy!

VI

Beside the cold water,
on the clear path
that obscure little tree
will some day give shade.
A white wood and four leaves, green,
that April hangs on the tree
the November wind takes away red.
Only a child would bite its fruit.
No one saw its flower. When does it bloom?
That little tree grows
only for a bird's landing,
soul of an instant—field and feathers—
a bird blue and petulant
that at the evening hour visits.

VII

How easy it is, how easy to fly!
All consists of not letting the ground
approach our feet. Valiant deed,
I fly, I fly, I fly!

VIII

To fly without wings where the sky is all!
Note this jolly thought:
To stop, to stop the world
between the tips of your feet,

y luego darle cuerda del revés,
para verlo girar en el vacío,
coloradito y frío,
y callado—no hay música sin viento—.
¡Claro, claro! ¡Poeta y cornetín
son de tan corto aliento!...
Sólo el silencio y Dios cantan sin fin.

IX

Pero caer de cabeza,
en esta noche sin luna,
en medio de esta maleza,
junto a la negra laguna...
*
—¿Tú eres Caronte, el fúnebre barquero?
Esa barba limosa..
                    —¿Y tú, bergante?
—Un fúnebre aspirante
de tu negra barcaza a pasajero,
que al lago irrebogable se aproxima.
—¿Razón?
              —La ignoro. Ahorcóme un peluquero.
—(Todos pierden memoria en este clima.)
—¿Delito?
              —No recuerdo.
                              —¿Ida, no más?
—¿Hay vuelta?
                  —Sí.
                              —Pues ida y vuelta, ¡claro!
—Sí, claro... y no tan claro: eso es muy caro.
Aguarda un momentín, y embarcarás.

X

¡Bajar a los infiernos como el Dante!
¡Llevar por compañero
a un poeta con nombre de lucero!
¡Y este fulgor violeta en el diamante!

and then to turn it in reverse,
to see it spinning in the void,
red and cold,
and hushed—there is no music without wind—.
Clearly! Flutist and poet
are of such short breath! . . .
Only God and silence sing without end.

IX

But to fall on your face,
on this night without moon,
in the middle of these weeds
by the black lagoon.

*

You are Charon, lugubrious ferryman?
That slimy beard. . .
    —And you, villain?
—A lugubrious neophyte
of your black passenger boat
approaching the lake that can't be crossed again.
—Reason?
    —I do not know. A barber hanged me.
—(All lose their memory in this clime.)
—Crime?
    —I do not recall.
      —One way only?
—Is there return?
    —Yes.
      —Then round trip, clearly!
—Yes, that is clear . . . and not so clear: it is very expensive.
Wait a moment, and you shall embark.

X

To descend to the infernal depths like Dante!
To take as companion
a poet named of a star!
And this violet brilliance in the diamond!

Dejad toda esperanza... Usted, primero.
¡Oh, nunca, nunca, nunca! Usted delante.

*

Palacios de mármol, jardín con cipreses,
naranjos redondos y palmas esbeltas.
Vueltas y revueltas,
eses y más eses.
"Calle del Recuerdo." Ya otra vez pasamos
por ella. "Glorieta de la Blanca Sor."
"Puerta de la Luna." Por aquí ya entramos.
"Calle del Olvido." Pero ¿adónde vamos
por estas molditas andurrias, señor?
                    —Pronto te cansas, poeta.
          —"Travesía del Amor"...
          ¡y otra vez la "Plazoleta
          del Desengaño Mayor"!

XI

—Es ella... Triste y severa.
Di, más bien, indiferente
como figura de cera.
                    *

—Es ella.. Mira y no mira.
—Pon el oído en su pecho
y, luego, dile: respira.

                    *

—No alcanzo hasta el mirador.
—Háblale.
                    —Si tu quisieras...
—Más alto.
                    —Dame esa flor.
¿No me respondes, bien mío?
¡Nada, nada!
Cuajadita con el frío
se quedó en la madrugada.

Abandon hope. . . You, first.
Oh, never, never, never! You, before.

*

Palaces of marble, garden of cypress,
round oranges, tall palms,
turnings and returnings,
reeling and staggering.
"Memory Street." Again we are passing
along it. "White Sister Square."
"Gate of the Moon." We enter here.
"Oblivion Street." But where do we go
on these cursed walks, sir?
    —Poet, soon you will tire.
    —"Passage of Love". . .
    and again the "Little Plaza
of the Great Disillusion"!

XI

—It is she. . . Severe and sad.
Or rather, indifferent
like a figure of wax.

*

—It is she. . . She looks and does not look.
—Put your ear on her breast
and then tell her: breathe.

*

—I don't reach the window.
—Speak to her.
    —If you like. . .
—Louder.
    —Give me that flower.
You do not answer, my love?
Nothing, nothing!
Stiff with cold
she was at dawn.

CLXXIII *Canciones a Guiomar*

I

No sabía
si era un limón amarillo
lo que tu mano tenía,
o el hilo de un claro día,
Guiomar, en dorado ovillo.
Tu boca me sonreía.

Yo pregunté. ¿Qué me ofreces?
¿Tiempo en fruto, que tu mano
eligió entre madureces
de tu huerta?

¿Tiempo vano
de una bella tarde yerta?
¿Dorada ausencia encantada?
¿Copia en el agua dormida?
¿De monte en monte encendida,
la alborada
verdadera?
¿Rompe en sus turbios espejos
amor la devanadera
de sus crepúsculos viejos?

II

En un jardín te he soñado,
alto, Guiomar, sobre el río,
jardín de un tiempo cerrado
con verjas de hierro frío.

Un ave insólita canta
en el almez, dulcemente,
junto al agua viva y santa,
toda sed y toda fuente.

En ese jardín, Guiomar,
el mutuo jardín que inventan
dos corazones al par,
se funden y complementan
nuestras horas. Los racimos

CLXXIII *Songs to Guiomar*

I

I did not know
if a yellow lemon it was
that you held in your hand,
or the thread of a clear day,
Guiomar, on a golden skein.
Your mouth smiled at me.

What do you offer me? I asked.
Time in fruit, chosen by your hand
from the ripeness
of your orchard trees?

Empty time
of a beautiful motionless evening?
Golden enchanted absence?
An image in the sleeping water?
From mountain to burning mountain
the true dawn?
Does love break in the turbid mirrors
the spool
of its ancient dusks?

II

In a garden, high over the river,
I have dreamed you, Guiomar,
a garden from a time since closed
by a grating of cold iron.

A rare bird is singing
sweetly in the lotus,
all thirst and all fountain
by the living sacred water.

In that garden, Guiomar,
the mutual garden born
of the joining of two hearts
our separate hours
into each other melt.
Together we press

de un sueño—juntos estamos—
en limpia copa exprimimos,
y el doble cuento olvidamos.

(Uno: Mujer y varón,
aunque gacela y león,
llegan juntos a beber.
El otro: No puede ser
amor de tanta fortuna:
dos soledades en una,
ni aun de varón y mujer.)

*

Por ti la mar ensaya olas y espumas,
y el iris, sobre el monte, otros colores,
y el faisán de la aurora canto y plumas,
y el búho de Minerva ojos mayores.
Por ti, ¡oh, Guiomar!...

III

Tu poeta
piensa en ti. La lejanía
es de limón y violeta,
verde el campo todavía.
Conmigo vienes, Guiomar;
nos sorbe la serranía.
De encinar en encinar
se va fatigando el día.
El tren devora y devora
día y riel. La retama
pasa en sombra; se desdora
el oro de Guadarrama.
Porque una diosa y su amante
huyen juntos, jadeante,
los sigue la luna llena.
El tren se esconde y resuena
dentro de un monte gigante.
Campos yermos, cielo alto.
Tras los montes de granito
y otros montes de basalto,

the clusters of grapes
from a dream into a glass,
and forget the double tale.

(One: Woman and man,
though gazelle and lion,
come together to drink.
The other: There cannot be
such a fortunate love:
two solitudes in one,
not even of man and woman.)

*

For you the sea tries waves and foam,
and the rainbow, over the mountain, other colors,
and the pheasant of the dawn, new feathers and song,
and the owl of Minerva, eyes that are greater.
For you, oh Guiomar! . . .

III

Your poet
is thinking of you, Guiomar.
The distance is of lemon and violet,
still green the countryside.
You are coming with me, Guiomar;
the mountains will swallow us.
From grove to oak grove,
the day weakens. And the train
goes devouring and devouring
the day and the rail.
The furze moves into shadow;
the Guadarrama is no longer gold.
For a goddess and her lover,
panting, flee together;
the full moon follows.
The train hides and resounds
inside the great mountain.
High sky, barren lands.
Beyond the mountains of granite
and mountains of basalt,

ya es la mar y el infinito.
Juntos vamos; libres somos.
Aunque el Dios, como en el cuento
fiero rey, cabalgue a lomos
del mejor corcel del viento,
aunque nos jure, violento,
su venganza,
aunque ensille el pensamiento,
libre amor, nadie lo alcanza.

*

Hoy te escribo en mi celda de viajero,
a la hora de una cita imaginaria.
Rompe el iris al aire el aguacero,
y al monte su tristeza planetaria.
Sol y campanas en la vieja torre.
¡Oh, tarde viva y quieta
que opuso al *panta rhei* su *nada corre*,
tarde niña que amaba tu poeta!
¡Y día adolescente
—ojos claros y músculos morenos—,
cuando pensaste a Amor, junto a la fuente,
besar tus labios y apresar tus senos!
Todo a esta luz de abril se transparenta;
todo en el hoy de ayer, el Todavía
que en sus maduras horas
el tiempo canta y cuenta,
se funde en una sola melodía,
que es un coro de tardes y de auroras.
A ti, Guiomar, esta nostalgia mía.

it is now the sea and the infinite.
We go together; we are free.
Although the God, a savage king,
may ride—as in the tale—
the best charger of the wind,
although, violent, he may swear
his vengeance on us from above,
although he may saddle thought,
nothing can touch free love.

*

Today I write you in my small compartment,
at the hour of an imaginary meeting.
The rainbow breaks the showers of the air
and the planetary sadness of the mountain.
Sun and bells in the old tower.
Oh, evening quiet and alive
that opposed the *panta rhei* with its *nothing flows*,
childlike evening that your poet loved!
And adolescent day
—dark muscles and clear eyes—,
when you had Love, next to the fountain,
kiss your lips and press your breast!
All becomes transparent in this April night;
all in the today of yesterday, the Yet
that in its mature hours
time sings and tells,
melts into a single melody,
a choir of evenings and dawns.
To you, this nostalgia of mine, Guiomar.

CLXXV Muerte de Abel Martín

Pensando que no veía
porque Dios no le miraba,
dijo Abel cuando moría:
Se acabó lo que se daba.
—J. DE MAIRENA: *Epigramas.*

I

Los últimos vencejos revolean
en torno al campanario;
los niños gritan, saltan, se pelean.
En su rincón, Martín el solitario.
¡La tarde, casi noche, polvorienta,
la algazara infantil, y el vocerío,
a la par, de sus doce en sus cincuenta!

*

¡Oh alma plena y espíritu vacío,
ante la turbia hoguera
con llama restallante de raíces,
fogata de frontera
que ilumina las hondas cicatrices!

*

Quien se vive se pierde, Abel decía.
¡Oh, distancia, distancia!, que la estrella
que nadie toca, guía.
¿Quién navegó sin ella?
Distancia para el ojo—¡oh lueñe nave!—,
ausencia al corazón empedernido,
y bálsamo suave
con la miel del amor, sagrado olvido.
¡Oh gran saber del cero del maduro
fruto, sabor que sólo el hombre gusta,
agua de sueño, manantial oscuro,
sombra divina de la mano augusta!
Antes me llegue, si me llega, el Día,
la luz que ve, increada,
ahógame esta mala gritería,
Señor, con las esencias de tu Nada.

CLXXV *The Death of Abel Martín*

Thinking that he could not see
because God was not watching him,
Abel said when he died:
What was given has come to an end.
—J. DE MAIRENA: *Epigrams*

I

The last swifts are circling
around the bell tower;
the children are skipping, shouting, fighting.
Martín the loner, in his usual corner.
The evening, turning into night, dusty,
the children's clamor, the shouting
of their twelve years in his fifty.

*

Oh soul whose spirit is empty,
before the turbid hearth
that holds a fire
crackling with roots,
a blaze illuminating deep scars!

*

He who lives is lost, Abel was saying.
Oh distance! the star
no one touches is guiding.
Who navigated without her?
Distance to the eye—oh faraway ship!—,
absence to the heart that is becoming like stone,
and balsam soft
with the honey of love, sacred oblivion.
Oh knowledge of the zero from the ripened fruit,
the taste known only to man,
water of dreams, a spring obscure,
divine shadow of the maginficent hand!
Before the Day arrives for me, if it arrives,
the uncreated light that sees,
Lord, drown this evil cry of mine
with the essence of your Nothingness.

II

El ángel que sabía
su secreto salió a Martín al paso.
Martín le dio el dinero que tenía.
¿Piedad? Tal vez. ¿Miedo al chantaje? Acaso.
Aquella noche fría
supo Martín de soledad; pensaba
que Dios no le veía,
y en su mudo desierto caminaba.

III

Y vio la musa esquiva,
de pie junto a su lecho, la enlutada,
la dama de sus calles, fugitiva,
la imposible al amor y siempre amada.
Díjole Abel: Señora,
por ansia de tu cara descubierta,
he pensado vivir hacia la aurora
hasta sentir mi sangre casi yerta.
Hoy sé que no eres tú quien yo creía;
mas te quiero mirar y agradecerte
lo mucho que me hiciste compañía
con tu frío desdén.
⠀⠀⠀⠀⠀⠀⠀⠀Quiso la muerte
sonreír a Martín, y no sabía.

IV

Viví, dormí, soñé y hasta he creado
—pensó Martín, ya turbia la pupila—
un hombre que vigila
el sueño, algo mejor que lo soñado.
Mas si un igual destino
aguarda al soñador y al vigilante,
a quien trazó caminos,
y a quien siguió caminos, jadeante,
al fin, sólo es creación tu pura nada,
tu sombra de gigante,
el divino cegar de tu mirada.

II

The angel who knew his secret
passed by Martín.
Martín gave him the money that he had.
Pity? Perhaps. Blackmail? Maybe.
That cold night
Martín knew solitude; he thought
that God was not seeing him,
and in his silent desert he walked.

III

And he saw the elusive muse,
in mourning, standing by his bed,
the lady of the streets, a fugitive,
impossible to love and loved always.
Abel said to her: Madam,
in desire to see your face unveiled
I have planned to live till dawn,
till my blood is still and I am pale.
Today I know you are not who I believed
you were; but I want to watch you for a while
and thank you for being my company somehow
with your cold disdain:
                Death tried to smile
at Martín, and did now know how.

IV

I lived, I slept, I dreamed,
and I've even created a man—thought Martín,
now cloudy his eye—a man who keeps guard
over the dream, which is better than the very dream.
But if the same destiny awaits
both the dreamer and the guard,
for whom he laid out roads,
and for whom he followed roads, breathing hard,
only your pure nothingness is creation in the end,
your shadow of a giant,
the divine blindness of your gaze.

V

—Y sucedío a la angustia la fatiga,
que siente su esperar desesperado,
la sed que el agua clara no mitiga,
la amargura del tiempo envenenado.
¡Esta lira de muerte!
                    Abel palpaba
su cuerpo enflaquecido.
¿El que todo lo ve no le miraba?
¡Y esta pereza, sangre del olvido!
¡Oh, sálvame, Señor!
                    Su vida entera,
su historia irremediable aparecía
escrita en blanda cera.
¿Y ha de borrarte el sol del nuevo día?
Abel tendió su mano
hacia la luz bermeja
de una caliente aurora de verano,
ya en el balcón de su morada vieja.
Ciego, pidió la luz que no veía.
Luego llevó, sereno,
el limpio vaso, hasta su boca fría,
de pura sombra—¡oh, pura sombra!—lleno.

CLXXVI *Otro clima*

¡Oh cámaras del tiempo y galerías
del alma ¡tan desnudas!,
dijo el poeta! De los claros días
pasan las sombras mudas.
Se apaga el canto de las viejas horas
cual rezo de alegrías enclaustradas;
el tiempo lleva un desfilar de auroras
con séquito de estrellas empañadas.
¿Un mundo muere? ¿Nace
un mundo? ¿En la marina
panza del globo hace
nueva nave su estela diamantina?

V

And the anguish was succeeded by fatigue,
fatigue that feels its hope become despair,
the thirst clear water does not quench,
the bitterness of poisoned time,
This lyre of death!
     Abel touched
his body grown thin.
Was not he who sees all watching him?
And this lethargy, blood of oblivion!
Oh, save me, Lord!
     His whole life,
his irremediable history,
written in soft wax, appeared.
And will it be erased by the sun of the new day?
Abel stretched out his hand
toward the red light glowing
of a hot summer dawn,
now on the balcony of his old abode.
Blind, he asked for the light he did not see.
And then, serene, he took
the clean glass, raised it to his cold mouth;
of pure shadow—oh, pure shadow!—it was full.

CLXXVI *Another Climate*

On naked halls of time
and galleries of the soul!
exclaimed the poet. From clear days
shadows mute come forth.
Like a prayer of cloistered joys
the song of old hours dies down;
with a retinue of fading stars
time carries away a parade of dawns.
A world dies? A world
is born? Does a new ship trace
across the ocean belly of the globe
its diamond wake?

¿Quillas al sol la vieja flota yace?
¿Es el mundo nacido en el pecado,
el mundo del trabajo y la fatiga?
¿Un mundo nuevo para ser salvado
otra vez? ¡Otra vez! Que Dios lo diga.
Calló el poeta, el hombre solitario,
porque un aire de cielo aterecido
le amortecía el fino estradivario.
Sangrábale el oído.
Desde la cumbre vio el desierto llano
con sombras de gigantes con escudos,
y en el verde fragor del océano
torsos de esclavos jadear desnudos.
Y un nihil de fuego escrito
tras de la selva huraña,
en áspero granito,
y el rayo de un camino en la montaña...

Keels to the sun, the old fleet lies still?
Is the world born in sin,
the world of fatigue, travail?
A new world to be saved again?
Again! Be it God's will.
The poet, solitary man,
grew quiet; for a hard wind
was deadening his violin.
His ear was bleeding.
From the peak he saw the desert plain
with shadows of giants carrying shields,
and naked torsos of panting slaves
in the roaring green of the sea.
And the sign of nothingness written
by fire in the rough granite
behind the forbidding forest,
and the ray of a road on the mountain. . .

LOS
COMPLEMENTARIOS
COMPLEMENTARY

CLXXXI *Los jardines del poeta*

A JUAN RAMÓN JIMÉNEZ

El poeta es jardinero. En sus jardines
corre sutil la brisa
con livianos acordes de violines,
llanto de ruiseñores,
ecos de voz lejana y clara risa
de jóvenes amantes habladores.
Y otros jardines tiene. Allí la fuente
le dice: Te conozco y te esperaba.
Y él, al verse en la onda transparente:
¡Apenas soy aquel que ayer soñaba!
Y otros jardines tiene. Los jazmines
añoran ya verbenas del estío,
y son liras de aroma estos jardines,
dulces liras que tañe el viento frío.
Y van pasando solitarias horas,
y ya las fuentes, a la luna llena,
suspiran en los mármoles, cantoras,
y en todo el aire sólo el agua suena.

CLXXXI *The Gardens of the Poet*

TO JUAN RAMÓN JIMÉNEZ

The poet is a gardener. In his garden
the breeze blows softly
with the nightingales' crying,
the violins' harmony,
echoes of distant voices and clear laughter
of young lovers speaking.
And he has other gardens. I know you
and I've awaited you, the fountain is saying.
And he, seeing himself in the transparent water:
Hardly am I the same who was yesterday dreaming!
And he has other gardens. The jasmine
recalls with nostalgia the summer verbena,
and those gardens are lyres of aromas,
sweet lyres that the cold wind is playing.
And solitary hours are passing,
and under the full moon the fountains
through the marble are breathing, singing,
and in all the air only the water sounds.

OTROS POEMAS
OTHER POEMS

CXCII *Simpatías*

Candidor postquam tondenti
barba cadebat.
VIRGILIO:
Egloga I.

¿Cúya es esta frente? ¿Cúyo
este mentón azulado?
¿Cúya esta boca sumida,
y estos ojos fatigados
de la letra diminuta
y de los montes lejanos?
Siempre mira el hombre al hombre
con piedad en su retrato.

CXCIII *Luz*

A DON MIGUEL DE UNAMUNO, EN PRUEBA
DE MI ADMIRACIÓN Y DE MI GRATITUD.

¿Será tu corazón un harpa al viento,
que tañe el viento?... Sopla el odio y suena
tu corazón; sopla tu corazón y vibra...
¡Lástima de tu corazón, poeta!
¿Serás acaso un histrión, un mimo
de mojigangas huecas?
¿No borrarán el tizne de tu cara
lágrimas verdaderas?
¿No estallará tu corazón de risa,
pobre juglar de lágrimas ajenas?

Mas no es verdad... Yo he visto
una figura extraña,
que vestida de luto—¡y cuán grotesca!—
vino un día a mi casa.
—"De tizne y albayalde hay en mi rostro
cuanto conviene a una doliente farsa;
yo te daré la gloria del poeta,
me dijo, a cambio de una sola lágrima."

CXCII *Sympathies*

Candidor postquam tondenti
barba cadebat.
Eclogue I
—VIRGIL

Whose is this brow?
Whose this bluish jaw?
Whose this sunken mouth,
and these eyes tired
from tiny print
and distant peaks.
Man always looks at man
with mercy in his face.

CXCIII *Light*

TO DON MIGUEL DE UNAMUNO, AS A TESTAMENT
TO MY ADMIRATION AND GRATITUDE.

Will your heart be a harp to the wind
that the wind plays? . . . Hate blows
and your heart sounds: your heart swells
and quivers. What a pity, poet!
Are you perhaps an actor, a mimic
of hollow masks? Will your face
be ever stained by paint
true tears will not erase?
Won't all those laughs make your heart explode,
poor juggler, whose tears are not your own?

But that is not true. . . I have seen
a strange and grotesque shape,
a figure in somber mourning dress,
who came to my house one day.
"There is enough soot and white lead on my face
for a troop of players to wear;
I will give you the glory of the poet
in exchange for a single tear."

Y otro día volvió a pedirme risa
que poner en sus hueras carcajadas. . .
—"Hay almas que hacen un bufón sombrío
de su histrión de alegres mojigangas.

Pero en tu alma de verdad, poeta,
sean puro cristal risas y lágrimas;
sea tu corazón arca de amores,
vaso florido, sombra perfumada."

And another day he asked for joy
to fill his loud and empty laughter.
"There are souls that make unhappy clowns
in their roles as gaily masked actors.
But, poet, in your soul that speaks the truth,
may your laughter and tears be of pure glass;
may your heart be a coffer of love,
perfumed shade, a flowering vase."